# LEIGHTON'S HIGH SIERRA CHECK DAM LEGACY

## A Photographic Journal

### STEVE D. BOWMAN

To order additional copies of this book, contact:
Xlibris Corporation
1-888-795-4274
www.Xlibris.com
Orders@Xlibris.com

# TABLE OF CONTENTS

# ACKNOWLEDGEMENTS

This project originated with a trip into the upper Emigrant Basin area in 1988 with James Gregg and Gene Powell. Subsequent trips to the Emigrant Wilderness furthered interest in Leighton's check dams in the eighteen years since. The recent controversy surrounding the check dams and the possibility that the check dams might be removed or let to decay naturally without maintenance was the driving cause to complete this work in its final form.

Many people have been instrumental in completing this project and this acknowledgement is however a short list. Many members of the family have been directly involved with the numerous backpacking and horse packing trips to the Emigrant Wilderness to gather additional information or in other activities and includes Robert and Janet Bowman, Gene Powell, James Gregg, John Gregg, and Edward and Elyn Gregg.

Brian Quelvog, of the California Department of Fish and Game (CDFG), who has been a long time advocate for maintaining and operating the check dams, provided numerous photographs and information related to the CDFG involvement in maintaining and operating the check dams.

Many original photographs reproduced here are part of the Leighton Photograph Collection that has been saved and cataloged by Bruce DeMott. Without Bruce's quick response several years ago to an inquiry from the Leighton family, these historic photographs most likely would have been lost forever. He also produced a 3-DVD disk set containing slide shows of the entire photograph collection that is an invaluable companion to this book.

Numerous historical photographs were also provided by the Tuolumne County Historical Society and Richard Camarena. Richard's help in locating these photographs and available information contributed significantly to this project.

Pam Conners, the Stanislaus National Forest Historian, provided numerous historical photographs and documents held by the forest's historical archives. Her involvement over many years was invaluable has allowed this project to be completed.

Tom Dahl, a local Sonora resident, provided a unique perspective on check dam construction by the Civilian Conservation Corps. Much of the historical documents related to this time period have become lost or were not retained. As a member of several check dam building crews, provided an interesting account of the construction and additional historical photographs.

During a fall backpacking trip to the Emigrant Wilderness to document and photograph the higher elevation check dams, one member of the party became ill and at the same time an unforeseen snow storm quickly descended. Unable to travel father, the group divided into two parties, with one staying behind in Kennedy Canyon and the other hiking to help through snowfall. Without the gracious help of Mono County Search and Rescue, including Jeff and Juta Holmquist and Barry, the Marine Corps Mountain Warfare Training Center, and Tuolumne County Search and Rescue, this project would not have been possible.

Martha Kearns, Brian Quelvog, Bruce DeMott, and Janet Bowman read the manuscript and eliminated numerous mistakes and provided helpful comment on this work.

# PREFACE

Outdoor enthusiasts discovering the Emigrant Wilderness of the high Sierra for the first time might easily consider it a pristine wilderness, rich in wildlife, streams, lakes, and scenic views. And yet, this is one area where the hand of man has worked to enrich the natural landscape. One of the most notable changes man has made in this area is the construction of small rock dams at the outlet of selected lakes and meadows. These dams were called *check dams* by Fred W. Leighton, who developed the concept of raising the water level of natural lakes and meadows for fishery and riparian enhancement. These check dams provide an enhanced habitat for mountain fish by providing additional water flow in the late summer months when natural streams typically run very low or completely dry. In addition, check dams at meadows were built to raise ground water levels within the meadows to provide enhanced forage for wildlife and stock. The check dams were built by hand with native rock gathered near the outlets of lakes and meadows and held together by mortar packed in by horse and mule.

Throughout Leighton's involvement in the check dam project, he stressed natural fisheries and conservation as portrayed in his statement that "*every recreationist who likes lakes and running streams and who believes in natural reproduction of a bountiful supply of trout and maintenance of fish life throughout the year, all at low cost, should insist on a comprehensive survey of the existing situation and establishment of check dams where required*" (Leighton, 1939). A 1939 article in the *Stockton Daily Evening Record* promoted Leighton's check dam conservation concept by highlighting the gains made during previous years proclaiming "*Cherry Creek and its tributaries are now living streams*" by "*maintaining some stream flow every day of the year*" as "*thousands of native Rainbow trout dies as a result*" of no water flow (1939). Leighton's comment on the success of the check dams at that time was "*the test has been made. It has proven the need for check dams all along the summit of the Sierra and such projects should hold high priority in conservation in California*" (1939), indicating his desire to continue the check dam project at other locations in the high Sierras.

This photographic journal chronicles the history and construction of the high Sierra check dams from the first one at Yellowhammer Lake in 1920 through the last one constructed at High Emigrant Lake in 1951, past the establishment of the Emigrant Wilderness in 1975, and through various stages of support and opposition which are on-going to this day. Each major period in either check dam construction or the period after is divided into separate chapters, with each check dam described in detail with historical and recent photographs, many that have never been published. Historical photographs, many of which have degraded through time, have been digitally restored as well as possible. Each check dam was individually photographed, measured, and documented in 2004 and/or 2005, except for Yellowhammer Lake. In addition, available historical writings and records of Fred Leighton and others were utilized to provide a more in-depth perspective on the check dams from those directly involved in construction and/or maintenance.

The many inspection trips, trips to gather support for the check dams, and information on the repair or reconstruction of the check dams have been described with the information that is available. Unfortunately, not all of the inspection trips or the many repairs made to the check dams could be described in this work due to a lack of information, clarity, or brevity. In addition, many records no longer exist, such as those associated with the Civilian Conservation Corps (CCC) involvement with check dams at Bear Lake and Y-Meadow.

Between 1920 and 1951, eighteen rock and mortar check dams were constructed at natural lakes and meadows within the Stanislaus National Forest, California in an area now designed as the Emigrant Wilderness. These check dams as envisioned by Fred W. Leighton, a nearby Sonora resident, would provide water storage and stream flows in the late summer, to enhance increased numbers of fisheries in the high Sierra. Many high Sierra lakes prior to this time were generally devoid of fish, and Leighton's ideas, along with stocking, would provide a viable fishery in the high Sierra. The check dams were built of native on-site stone and packed-in mortar with the exception of check dams at Yellowhammer, Leighton and Red Can Lakes, which were generally constructed as earthen embankments. Leighton's check dam ideas were built upon conservation values and to develop naturally reproducing fisheries, rather than larger, more environmentally invasive projects that were typical in the early 1900's.

The eighteen check dams were built in the high Sierra of the Stanislaus National Forest (SNF) in an area that would ultimately become the Emigrant Wilderness. The 113,088 acre Emigrant Wilderness is located entirely within the SNF and is bordered to the south by Yosemite National Park, to the east by the Toiyabe National Forest and West Hoover Wilderness Planning Area, to the north by State Highway 108 and SNF forest lands, and to the west by SNF forest lands. The northeastern portion of the wilderness area is characterized by sparsely vegetated volcanic ridges and glaciated valleys. The remainder of the wilderness area is generally sparsely to moderately vegetated granitic ridges and glaciated valleys with numerous meadows and lakes and lies in one of the most unique areas within the high Sierra.

Fred Leighton at Camp Yellowhammer corral in 1971 with characteristic wooden stump used for mounting his horse (Courtesy of Ernie Marino).

Three types of check dams would eventually be constructed: streamflow maintenance dams to provide streamflow throughout the summer, lake level maintenance dams to provide additional water storage, and meadow maintenance dams to provide sub-irrigation of high country meadows. Leighton's first dam at Yellowhammer Lake in 1920 was intended as a lake level maintenance dam and was constructed by Leighton and his friend, Bill Burnham. Leighton and Burnham also constructed dams at Red Can Lake and Leighton Lake. The first streamflow maintenance dam was constructed at Leighton Lake in 1925. The first meadow maintenance dam was constructed at Horse Meadow between 1934 and 1935.

The suggested flows released through gate valves on the check dams were frequently measured in Miner's Inches, a unit no longer frequently used. One Miner's Inch equals approximately 1.5 cubic feet of water per minute [cfm] (Sizes, 2005) or 11.2 gallons per minute [gpm].

In the early 1930's, Leighton gathered interest from Tuolumne County sportsmen, conservationists, and others who constructed dams at Long Lake, Bigelow Lake, Emigrant Meadow Lake, Lower Buck Lake, and Emigrant Lake. Starting in 1933 during the Great Depression, the U. S. Forest Service (USFS) became interested in check dam construction and enlisted the help of the Civilian Conservation Corps (CCC) who had a work camp nearby at Pinecrest. The USFS and the CCC ultimately built eight check dams at Y Meadow, Bear Lake, Horse Meadow, Cow Meadow Lake, Huckleberry Lake, Snow Lake, Cooper Meadow, and Whitesides Meadow. The final two dams to be constructed were built in 1951 at Middle Emigrant Lake and High Emigrant Lake and were jointly constructed by the USFS and the California Department of Fish and Game (CDFG). By the 1950's, support for additional check dams was lacking, and no new check dams would be built in the high Sierra of the Stanislaus National Forest.

The Emigrant Wilderness was designated on January 3, 1975 (USFS, 2003) by incorporating the 98,043 acre Emigrant Basin Primitive Area and other areas adjacent to the primitive area as directed by the federal Wilderness Act of 1964. As part of the wilderness planning process, an Emigrant Wilderness Management Plan was prepared in 1979 by the U. S. Forest Service that required a study to determine the condition, value, environmental impact, and cost effectiveness of the check dams (USFS, 1979). This plan did not specifically state whether or not to keep the check dams. The study, in the form of an environmental assessment (EA) was completed in November, 1989 after five years of work. At that time, Blaine Cornell, the Stanislaus Forest Supervisor, signed a Decision Notice that called for phasing out of 6 dams and retaining the remaining 12 dams; however, this decision was appealed by the California Wilderness Coalition (CWC) and others. In 1984, an additional 6,100 acres was added to the Emigrant Wilderness (USFS, 2003), resulting in the current size and extent of the wilderness area.

| Check Dam Location | Date Constructed | Constructed By | Major Repair Date | Type | Number of Dams |
|---|---|---|---|---|---|
| Yellowhammer Lake | 1920 | Leighton/Burnham | 1977 | LL | 1 |
| Red Can Lake | 1921 | Leighton/Burnham | --- | LL | 1 |
| Leighton Lake | 1925 | Leighton/Burnham | 1976 | SM | 1 |
| Long Lake | 1931 | Leighton and others | 1955, 1981 | SM | 8 |
| Bigelow Lake | 1931 | Leighton and others | 1951, 1953-54, 1964 | SM | 4 |
| Emigrant Meadow Lake | 1931 | Leighton and others | 1952 | SM | 1 |
| Lower Buck Lake | 1931 | Leighton and others | 1954, 1968-70, 1974 | SM | 1 |
| Emigrant Lake | 1931 | Leighton and others | 1934, 1952 | SM | 1 |
| Y-Meadow Dam | 1933-1934 | CCC/USFS | 1964 | SM | 1 |
| Bear Lake | 1933 | CCC/USFS | --- | SM | 1 |
| Horse Meadow | 1934 | CCC | 1960 | MM | 1 |
| Cow Meadow Lake | 1934 | USFS/CCC | 1980 | LL | 4 |
| Huckleberry Lake | 1934 | CCC | 1971 | SM | 9 |
| Snow Lake | 1934 | CCC | 1953-54 | SM | 11 |
| Cooper Meadow | 1940 | CCC | --- | MM | 1 |
| Whitesides Meadow | 1941 | CCC | 1985-85 | MM | 1 |
| Middle Emigrant Lake | 1951 | USFS/CDFG | --- | SM | 1 |
| High Emigrant Lake | 1951 | USFS/CDFG | 1955, 1958 | SM | 1 |

Type Code: LL = Lake Level Maintenance, SM = Streamflow Maintenance, and MM = Meadow Maintenance.
(USFS, 2003; Conners, 1986; Quelvog, 1986).

In September 2003, the SNF published a Draft Environmental Impact Statement (DEIS) related to the check dams in the Emigrant Wilderness that evaluated several management alternatives, including Alternative 1: *maintaining 12 dams and allowing six to deteriorate naturally*, Alternative 2: *no action*, and Alternative 3: *maintaining seven dams eligible for listing on the National Register of Historic Places and allowing the remainder to deteriorate naturally*. On December 16, 2003, the SNF Forest Supervisor published a Record of Decision (ROD) based on the DEIS, that selected a modified Alternative 1 in providing maintenance of Red Can Dam and allowing Cow Meadow and Y-Meadow dams to deteriorate naturally (USFS, 2003). On February 2, 2004, the Central Sierra Environmental Resource Center and Wilderness Watch, environmental special interest groups, and the Tuolumne County Board of Supervisors filed an appeal of the decision in which the two environmental groups requested Alternative 2 (no action) and Tuolumne County requested more check dams be placed on the maintenance list. On March 18, 2004 the Acting Deputy Regional Forester affirmed the previous Forest Supervisors decision as appropriate and allowed the SNF to implement the decision after April 2, 2004.

Unsatisfied with the decision and appeal denial, the High Sierra Hikers Association (HSHA) and Wilderness Watch, in a joint civil case, filed suit against the USFS on August 20, 2004 in U. S. District Court, San Francisco alleging the USFS violated the Wilderness Act, the National Forest Management Act, and the National Environmental Policy Act and to prevent the USFS from maintaining or operating any of the check dams (HSHA v. USFS, 2004). In a November, 2004 response to the complaint brought forward in the suit, the USFS stated the HSHA had not *"exhausted its administrative remedies"* and that the suit should be *"dismissed for its improper venue"* (HSHA v. USFS, 2004).

As the Northern District Court of California agreed with the defendants (USFS and interveners) motion to dismiss for the improper venue (location) and the failure of the plaintiffs (HSHA and others) to exhaust administrative remedies, the Court transferred the case to the Eastern District of California on April 8, 2005 (HSHA v. USFS, 2005) and dismissed the High Sierra Hikers Association from the case due to its failure in exhausting administrative remedies, such as the appeal process.

The case is yet unresolved as of June, 2006 and the controversy will surely continue. As delays continue in resolving the maintenance and operation of all 18 check dams, further vandalism and decay due to the severe winter weather present in the Emigrant Basin take their toll on the check dams. If these issues cannot be resolved soon, it is likely that many of the check dams will deteriorate significantly beyond reasonable repair and the region will have lost another historical connection to our past. In addition, an important recreational fishery in the high Sierra will be impacted.

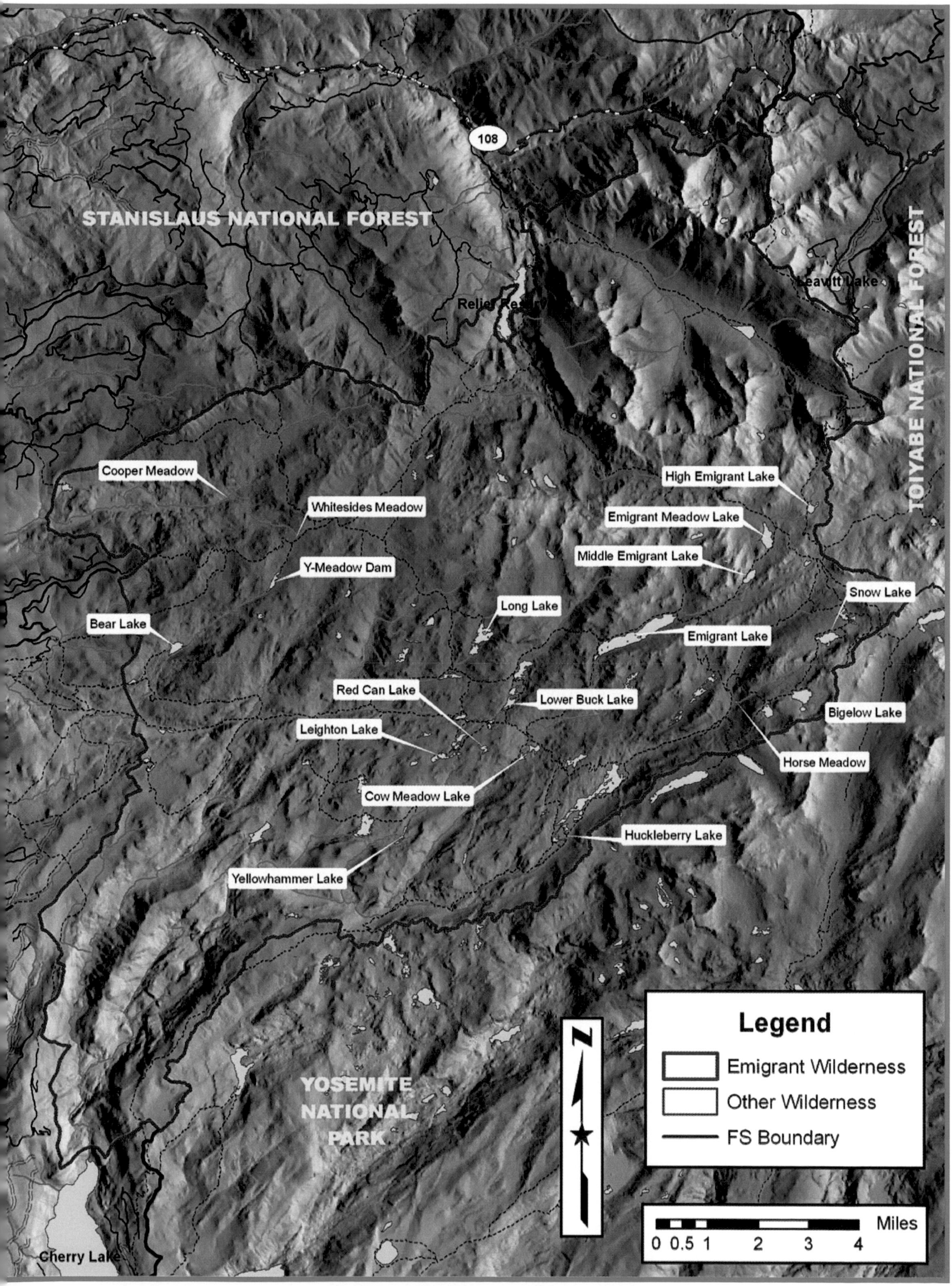

STANISLAUS NATIONAL FOREST

108

Relief Res

Leavitt Lake

TOIYABE NATIONAL FOREST

Cooper Meadow

Whitesides Meadow

Y-Meadow Dam

High Emigrant Lake

Emigrant Meadow Lake

Middle Emigrant Lake

Long Lake

Snow Lake

Emigrant Lake

Bear Lake

Red Can Lake

Lower Buck Lake

Leighton Lake

Bigelow Lake

Horse Meadow

Cow Meadow Lake

Huckleberry Lake

Yellowhammer Lake

YOSEMITE NATIONAL PARK

Cherry Lake

### Legend

Emigrant Wilderness

Other Wilderness

—— FS Boundary

N

Miles

0 0.5 1    2    3    4

# THE DRY EMIGRANT BASIN AND THE FIRST CHECK DAMS
## (1896 – 1925)

Fred W. Leighton's check dam ideas began in the summer of 1896, when he accompanied his uncle, Alvoh Shaw, who was hired by Dave Rosassco, to drive cattle during the summer in the area of the high Sierra now known as the Emigrant Wilderness. During these times in the high Sierra, Leighton "*watched streams and large canyons gradually go dry as the snow pack disappeared*" (Leighton, 1969). These streams and canyons included the East, West, and North Forks of Cherry Creek. During that summer, Leighton observed that there were no fish in the Emigrant Basin and that Shaw wanted to find rainbow trout to stock local streams, as the trout might "*congregate in the few larger holes for survival during the year when the stream completely dried up*" (Leighton, 1969). Leighton and Shaw later rode to Coffin Hollow along Lily Creek with several five-gallon oil cans to collect trout they later released in Louse Canyon along the West Fork of Cherry Creek. This was the first documented occurrence of fish stocking in the Emigrant Basin (Leighton, 1969); however, some stocking may have occurred earlier by sheepherders (USFS, 2003). Later in 1897, Shaw who was camped at Piute Meadows, packed fish for stocking in coal-oil cans from Coffin Hollow to Louse Canyon, Deer Lake, Buck Lakes, Wood Lake, Jewelry Lake, and Emigrant Lake (Leighton, 1969). Guy Scott, a California state game warden, packed fish into Pingree Lake and Big Lake sometime after 1910; however, this stocking was reported to be unsuccessful.

The next year in 1897, Leighton worked for Dave Rosassco driving cattle to the old Rosassco Camp, now called Camp Yellowhammer. During July, Leighton observed that all the streams he passed were full of water (Leighton, 1969) as they had been in the early to mid summer in previous years. In September 1903, while deer hunting at Hells Hole on the West Fork of Cherry Creek and at Hyatt Lake, Leighton observed no flow in the West Fork of Cherry Creek or in Cherry Creek below Hyatt Lake (Leighton, 1969).

After graduation from the Poverty Hill School in Stent in 1900, Leighton went to work for the Jumper Mine as a mill car attendant (Marovich, 1977). Later, in 1909 Leighton married Edna Hales, the daughter of the founding partner of the Hales and Symons Company in Sonora. Leighton returned to the Sonora area in 1914 after additional schooling in San Francisco and worked for the Union Construction Company that was building the Camp 9 powerhouse and Relief Dam in the high Sierra above Sonora.

Camp Yellowhammer area in summer 1990.

Leighton's long absence from the Emigrant Basin ended in September 1917 when he and his wife packed into Cow Meadow and Lord Meadow along the North Fork of Cherry Creek. At this time, Leighton observed no flow in Cherry Creek, repeating a pattern of no to low stream flows in late summer. This trip would be one of many summer trips into the Emigrant Basin he would organize throughout his life. On September 3, 1919, Leighton and his friend Bill Burnham, owner of Burnham's Candy Store in Sonora, applied for a permit to the Stanislaus National Forest for a camp site and horse range at the old Rosassco Camp, which he then named Yellowhammer Camp for the nearby Yellowhammer Lake. This camp would be used as a base camp for the many check dam inspection trips Leighton would organize along with numerous friends and acquaintances.

Camp Yellowhammer sign (summer 1990).

During 1919, Leighton again observed dry streams in the Emigrant Basin, and during the 1920's the streams were generally dry, except for a small flow of water from Hyatt Lake. The flow from Hyatt Lake, Leighton observed, was from water stored from *"a self made check dam"* (Leighton, 1969) that was discharged through a small, natural opening in the rock. Flow from Hyatt Lake kept small pools in Cherry Creek full as far downstream as Cherry Valley (now inundated by Cherry Lake). The observation of natural water storage and slow release was the foundation on which Leighton based his check dam conservation concept. During the early 1920's, on fishing trips from Hulls Meadow where Leighton had a cabin, Leighton found the Clavey River dry above the confluence of Two Mile Creek on several occasions and that Two Mile Creek was the only stream for the Clavey River (Leighton, 1972).

In 1920, Leighton and Burnham built the first check dam at the outlet of a small un-named lake at that time that was later named Yellowhammer Lake by Leighton (Burghduff, 1933). This check dam would raise the lake level a few feet and would later be referred to as a lake level dam.

Stocking of lakes with fish at this time was very difficult, due to the poor existing trails, rough country, and distance from suitable lakes or streams with fish to the west. Some stocking of lakes in the Emigrant Basin was made by others, packing native fish gathered at Laurel Lake (Burghduff, 1933), now within Yosemite National Park. Leighton also packed fish from Louse Canyon to stock Yellowhammer Lake in 1919 and from Buck Meadows to stock Yellowhammer Lake in 1920 (Leighton, 1963, 1977). The next year in 1921, Leighton and Burnham constructed a second check dam at Red Can Lake, upstream from Yellowhammer Lake.

The problem now faced by Leighton was to provide a self-sufficient fishery at Yellowhammer Lake. Since the stream entering Yellowhammer Lake went dry in mid to late summer, spawning grounds were limited. Then in 1925, Leighton and Burnham completed a third check dam at 50 Acre Lakes, now named Leighton Lake, to provide stream flow above Yellowhammer Lake, by *"working a few days each vacation"* (Leighton, 1977). This was the first dam intended for stream flow augmentation, termed streamflow maintenance by Leighton. Leighton wrote that in 1925, stream flow through Yellowhammer Lake was due to the check dam they constructed earlier at Leighton Lake (Leighton, 1969). Construction of check dams at Yellowhammer and Leighton Lakes resulted in increased fish spawning grounds that would allow for a self-sufficient fishery in the area to develop. The success of fishery enhancement at these lakes would lead to additional check dams constructed in the Emigrant Basin.

The three original check dams were all generally earthen embankments that could easily be constructed by two people and were intended to support a natural fishery at Yellowhammer Lake. This early attempt at check dams, as Leighton referred to them, would form the foundation for fifteen other rock and mortar check dams to be constructed within the Emigrant Basin between 1931 and 1951 and other check dams constructed by the Mt. Ralston Fish Planting Club in the Desolation Basin area west of Lake Tahoe.

# YELLOWHAMMER LAKE

Fred Leighton and Bill Burnham constructed the first check dam in the Emigrant Basin area at Yellowhammer Lake in 1920 as an earthen embankment that would function as a lake level check dam. This check dam was intended to provide fish habitat at the lake, in that earlier fish stocking attempts were generally unsuccessful. In 1977, Jim Freeman and Andy Weaver of the California Department of Fish and Game reinforced the check dam (Quelvog, 1986).

**Quick Facts**

| | |
|---|---|
| Date Constructed: | 1920 |
| Constructed By: | Leighton & Burnham |
| Check Dam Type: | Lake Level |
| Check Dams: | 1 |
| Valve System: | None |
| Waterflow Weir: | Unknown |
| Lake Size: | 20 Acres |
| Drainage: | Cherry Creek |
| Elevation: | 7,723 feet |
| Date Repaired: | 1977 |

Yellowhammer Lake check dam in summer 1990. Flow from left to right obscured by fallen logs.

| Dam | Date | Type | Length (ft) | Height (ft) | | Width (ft) | |
|---|---|---|---|---|---|---|---|
| | | | | Upstream | Downstream | Top | Base |
| Total | As Constructed | Main | ? | ? | ? | ? | ? |

Yellowhammer Canal, date unknown (Leighton Collection Photograph, Courtesy of Bruce DeMott).

Edna Leighton at Yellowhammer Lake, date unknown (Leighton Collection Photograph, Courtesy of Bruce DeMott).

Yellowhammer Lake check dam 8/1993 (Courtesy of Brian Quelvog).

Yellowhammer Lake in summer 1990.

# RED CAN LAKE

Leighton and Bill Burnham constructed a check dam at Red Can Lake in 1921 as a lake level dam. The inlet stream to Yellowhammer Lake would often go dry, causing fish kill that Leighton wanted to reduce by providing stream flow from upstream lakes. However, as this was a lake level dam, flow upstream of Yellowhammer Lake mainly originates from Leighton Lake. This check dam was constructed as an earthen embankment in the same manner as the Yellowhammer Lake check dam.

Currently, the Red Can Lake check dam is in poor condition, since a tree growing into the check dam has fallen over, as shown below. Water seeping through the check dam flows down numerous cracks in the exposed glacier-polished granite, creating numerous small, picturesque waterfalls.

### Quick Facts

| | |
|---|---|
| Date Constructed: | 1921 |
| Constructed By: | Leighton & Burnham |
| Check Dam Type: | Lake Level |
| Check Dams: | 1 |
| Valve System: | None |
| Water flow Weir: | None |
| Lake Size: | 8 Acres |
| Drainage: | Cherry Creek |
| Elevation: | 8,296 Feet |
| Date Repaired: | Unknown |

Red Can Lake check dam in summer 2005 showing damage from fallen pine tree.

| Dam | Date | Type | Length (ft) | Height (ft) | | Width (ft) | |
|---|---|---|---|---|---|---|---|
| | | | | Upstream | Downstream | Top | Base |
| Total | As Constructed | Main | ? | ? | ? | ? | ? |
| 1 | 8/4/2005 | Main | 8 | 1-1/2 – 2 | 2 | 2 | 2 |

Red Can Lake in summer 2005 looking towards outlet and the canyon of the North Fork of Cherry Creek.

Outlet area of Red Can Lake in summer 2005. Single check dam to left of blue backpack. Excess water flows over glacier polished granite in foreground, through water stained area.

Red Can Lake in summer 2005.

Red Can Lake check dam before fallen tree, 8/1984 (Courtesy of Brian Quelvog).

# LEIGHTON LAKE

Fred Leighton and Bill Burnham constructed a second earthen check dam at the outlet of Leighton Lake (then called 50 Acre Lake) in 1925 as a streamflow maintenance check dam. This check dam was constructed to provide additional storage of water for release downstream to Yellowhammer Lake to reduce fish kill due to low or no flow in the Yellowhammer Lake inlet stream area.

An inspection trip by the California Department of Fish & Game (CDFG) in 1956 observed some damage from flow over the top of the dam; otherwise the check dam was generally in good condition (Lewis, 1956). New outlet pipe and trash racks were installed by Andy Weaver, of the CDFG in 1976 along with removing or cabling off sunken logs.

### Quick Facts

| | |
|---|---|
| Date Constructed: | 1925 |
| Constructed By: | Leighton & Burnham |
| Check Dam Type: | Streamflow Maintenance |
| Check Dams: | 1 |
| Valve System: | Slide Gate |
| Water flow Weir: | None Known |
| Lake Size: | 25 Acres |
| Drainage: | Cherry Creek |
| Elevation: | 8,279 Feet |
| Date Repaired: | 1976 |

Leighton Lake check dam in summer 2005. Slide gate and trash rack centrally located in check dam and spillway to left of photograph.

| Dam | Date | Type | Length (ft) | Height (ft) | | Width (ft) | |
|---|---|---|---|---|---|---|---|
| | | | | Upstream | Downstream | Top | Base |
| Total | As Constructed | Main | 30 | 7 | ? | 2 | ? |
| 1 | 8/4/2005 | Main | 46* | 2.3 | 6 | 4 | ? |

\* - 35 foot main dam section with 11 foot long spillway section, actively eroded

Leighton Lake check dam in summer 2005. Actively eroding spillway at far end of check dam. Valve pipe outlet obscured by brush below central section of check dam. Slide valve is mounted in a downstream position, rather than in a submerged, upstream position as the other check dam valves. This valve, pipe, and trash rack system is unique to all of the check dams.

An inspection trip in 2005 found the Leighton Lake check dam in generally good condition, except for the spillway. Erosion of the spillway is undermining a large granite boulder that if left unchecked, could undermine to the point that the boulder would fall into the spillway. In addition, further erosion of the spillway could cause erosion of the check dam above. Very little leakage through the dam was observed, except for a damp area at the eastern end of the check dam and primarily at the smooth interface to granite bedrock. Extensive brush growth is present along the outlet stream.

Future maintenance activities will likely consist of stabilization of the spillway, removal of log snags on and above the check dam, and cleaning of the inlet grate. Eventual replacement of the slide gate will also be required due to rust damage.

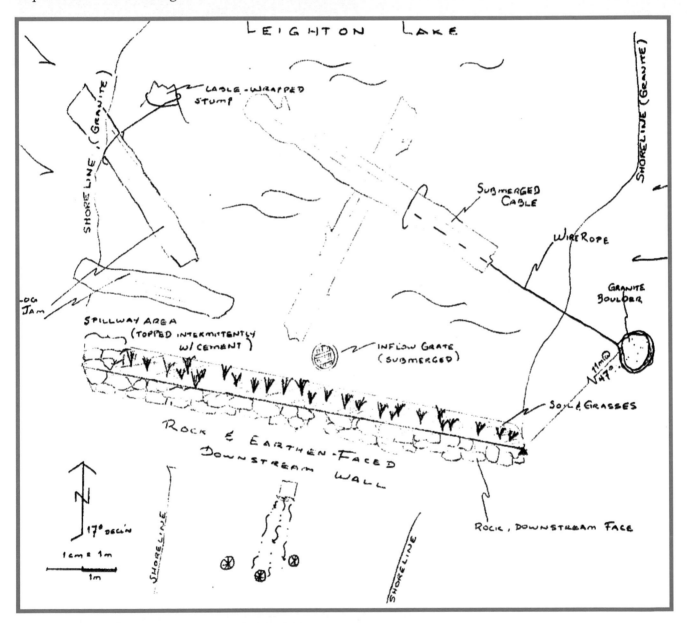

Leighton Lake Check Dam Sketch (Modified from and courtesy of Conners, 1986).

Leighton Lake check dam in 1928 with Fred Leighton at left, Karl DeFiebre, and L. Fraguero (Courtesy of the Tuolumne County Historical Society). Original photograph on file at TCHS is incorrectly labeled as Yellowhammer Dam. Spillway area at far end of dam shows little erosion at this time.

Unique Leighton Lake check dam slide gate on downstream side of check dam (8/4/2005).

View of Leighton Lake looking south towards check dam (8/4/2005).

Fred Leighton at Leighton Lake check dam in September, 1971 (Courtesy of Ernie Marino).

Leighton Lake check dam in October, 1984 with significant log debris. Spillway area appears to be in generally good condition (Courtesy of Brian Quelvog).

Leighton Lake check dam, date unknown. Man standing on outlet works. Two trees in background are no longer present (Courtesy of Brian Quelvog).

# TUOLUMNE COUNTY CONSERVATIONISTS TEAM WITH LEIGHTON (1930 – 1931)

With the success of check dams at Yellowhammer, Red Can, and Leighton Lakes, Leighton continued his efforts toward constructing additional check dams in the high Sierra by gathering support from local interests in Tuolumne County and the U. S. Forest Service. This stage of dam construction was the result of Leighton's grass roots efforts for support and would eventually result in the construction of check dams at Long, Bigelow, Emigrant Meadow, Lower Buck, and Emigrant Lakes with the help of the local community and others.

On September 2, 1930, Leighton organized an inspection trip to the Emigrant Basin to promote his check dam concept, locate suitable check dam sites, and plan for their future construction. This would be one of many inspection trips Leighton would organize to promote his check dam ideas. The 1930 inspection trip consisted of J.R. Hall the Stanislaus National Forest Supervisor at that time; J. A. Carey, Stanislaus National Forest Ranger, A. E. Burghduff of the California Division of Fish & Game; Harry Cole, Basin Creek Hatchery Foreman; Frank Kurzi, Kennedy Meadows Pack Station Owner; and Fred W. Leighton representing the Tuolumne County Fish & Game Association (Leighton, 1969). Leighton took the party to Camp Yellowhammer and Leighton Lake where he and Bill Burnham had constructed earthen check dams several years earlier.

As Leighton stated, the trip was *"to go into the Emigrant Basin to see the suggested locations, estimate their value to streamflow maintenance, for wildlife and the beautification of the three canyons"* (Leighton, 1969). During this trip, the party observed that all of the upper reaches of Cherry Creek were dry, except for small pools in meadows, and that numerous trout were stranded in these pools (Burghduff, 1933). After the trip, A. E. Burghduff commented that the area was well suited for a fishery: *"this inaccessible high granite area with its myriad of lakes, most of which appear well suited for trout, will, if properly stocked, provide a great amount of angling"* and noted that *"the streams are dry during the late summer"* (Burghduff, 1930).

It was during this time that Leighton enlisted the help of the California Department of Fish & Game, including A. E. Burghduff and Harry Cole. Harry Cole, a member of the inspection party, was a foreman at the Basin Creek Hatchery that was located at the confluence of Basin Creek and the North Fork of the Tuolumne River east of the community of Tuolumne.

California Department of Fish & Game (CDFG) Basin Creek Hatchery on the North Fork of the Tuolumne River (1934) (Leighton Collection Photograph, Courtesy of Bruce DeMott).

After inspecting the check dams Leighton and Burnham had built earlier and the proposed check dam sites at Emigrant, Emigrant Meadow, Snow, Long, and Upper and Lower Buck Lakes, the party *"was unanimous in a decision that the most inexpensive and permanently constructed dam would be one built of rock with enough concrete used in between the rocks near the face of the dam to make it water tight"* (Leighton, 1969). This new concept of check dam construction would form the basis of all new check dam construction in the Emigrant Basin.

To initiate the construction of additional check dams in the Emigrant Basin, Leighton organized several meetings with the state Chamber of Commerce and sportsmen's groups to raise support and funding. Leighton also enlisted the help of M. M. O'Shaughnessy, the City of San Francisco city engineer who lead construction of Hetch Hetchy Reservoir seven years earlier. O'Shaughnessy gave his support to Leighton in 1931, stating he would "*do everything possible to urge the consummation of* [his] *plans*". In addition, he thought Leighton's check dam ideas were "*too moderate*" (O'Shaughnessy, 1931). Based on his background of water storage for power and drinking water supplies, O'Shaughnessy thought larger dams and an access road built from Relief Reservoir to the north could be constructed, even though significantly larger dams and an access road would have been overkill for Leighton's plan to protect fish in streams. Leighton's reply agreed more dams should be constructed but that larger storage was not needed for his plan and that an agreement with the Forest Service could be made by packing in of men and materials from Kennedy Meadows without the construction of an access road (Leighton, 1931), reinforcing the conservation and fisheries ethic he promoted.

Leighton organized additional meetings with the U. S. Forest Service, Tuolumne County, California Division of Fish & Game, and the City and County of San Francisco to raise support and needed funding for check dam construction. The result of these meetings was the show of support for the project through the contribution of $1,000 each from the California Division of Fish & Game, the City and County of San Francisco, and Tuolumne County. J. R. Hall, the Stanislaus National Forest Supervisor, donated the use of camp equipment and transportation for the men and supplies. In addition, the Pacific Gas & Electric Company donated used cable and riveted pipe, Hales and Symons Lumber (Leighton was then employed as the company secretary) donated a one slips scraper, snatch block, and a pick; Frank Dondero donated a one slip scraper; Leighton donated his time as foreman of construction; and numerous others donated tools and supplies totaling approximately $1,619 to the check dam construction effort. These donations and plans eventually resulted in the construction of five

check dams thus providing "*five large lakes to be raised to provide water storage to maintain stream flow in the four large canyons and Cherry River* [Creek] *down to where it joins the water flowing from Lake Eleanor, a combined distance of about 75 miles*" (Leighton, 1931). The distance of 75 miles of stream flow maintenance was later reduced due to the construction of Cherry Reservoir in 1955.

Due to the requirement for a state dam construction permit, Leighton organized another trip to the Emigrant Basin in August, 1931, so that W. A. Perkins, the State Engineer and Robert Strauch, the Tuolumne County Surveyor, could inspect the proposed check dam sites. Both Robert Strauch and the state Division of Water Resources agreed to donate their services in securing the needed state dam permits. The trip also included J. R. Hall, Joe Cademartori, a mining engineer, Leland Gibbs, M. Petersons, and Frank Kurzi. During this inspection trip, it was decided by the party not to construct a check dam at Upper Buck Lake as the proposed five foot high dam "*would not raise the water high enough to back water far enough up the meadow to save the hatch of fish that takes place there each year*" and to construct a check dam at the larger Bigelow Lake instead of Snow Lake which would be cheaper to build (Leighton, 1931).

Leighton organized two crews of seven men each to construct check dams during the summer of 1931. The first crew consisted of Frank Moyle (Foreman), Ralph McMahon, Roy Whitto (Cook), J. McGinnis, Elmer Shaw, A. J. Freitas, and Bill Burnham. The second crew consisted of George B. Connally (Foreman), Paul Novelli, Chas Wight, M. V. Brooks, John Gerber, Clarence Maddox, and Joe Bolognesi (Leighton, 1963). Check dams at Bigelow Lake, Emigrant Lake, and Emigrant Meadow Lake were constructed by the first crew starting on August 24, 1931. Check dams at Lower Buck Lake and Long Lake were constructed by the second crew starting on August 27, 1931. Both crews, members of the Tuolumne County Fish & Game Association, finished construction on October 4, 1931 under Leighton's supervision. During check dam construction, Leighton ran a "*five horse poney express between the two camps*" moving supplies as needed (Leighton, 1931).

August, 1931 Engineers Tour and Survey with Robert Strauch, W. A. Perkins, Jess Hall, Joe Cademartori, Lee Gibbs, Pete Peterson, Frank Korzi, Fred Leighton, and Hubbs Grave (Leighton Collection Photograph, Courtesy of Bruce DeMott).

August, 1931 Engineers Tour and Survey with Robert Strauch, W. A. Perkins, Jess Hall, Joe Cademartori, Lee Gibbs, Pete Peterson, Frank Korzi, Fred Leighton, and Hubbs Grave. Taken by W. A. Perkins at Summit Meadow (Leighton Collection Photograph, Courtesy of Bruce DeMott).

The $3,000 raised earlier by Leighton did not cover all the expenses incurred during check dam construction and was exhausted by the time each work crew was about half-way through their last check dam. The budget was short $669 in actual expenses (Leighton, 1931). The actual cost of the five check dams built in 1931 was $5,067, including the value of donated supplies and labor (Leighton, 1931). Leighton got the men to agree to continue work and finish construction on the last two check dams and then they would be paid when additional funds were available. The shortage of funds was eventually paid off between 1932 and 1934 from donations from the Tuolumne County Board of Supervisors, California Fish and Game Commission, and a Sportsman's dance and rally (Leighton, 1931).

# LONG LAKE

A series of check dams at Long Lake were constructed in 1931 by Leighton and a work crew headed by Geo Connally as a streamflow maintenance dam on a tributary to Buck Meadow Creek. A total of one main dam and seven saddle dams were constructed. Check dams at Long Lake impound additional water for release all summer long, flowing down to Deer Lake and Jewelry Lake before flowing into Buck Meadows Creek and the West Fork of Cherry Creek. This is one of the more scenic views in the Emigrant Basin. Several large schools of trout were visible in the large pools below the main, valved check dam in July, 2005. It was pools such as these at Long Lake that Leighton observed would frequently go dry due to low or no flow in late summer

The dam was reconstructed in 1955, an instruction plate was installed in 1970, and the valve cleared of rocks and repairs made to the check dams in 1981 by the California Department of Fish & Game (CDFG) (Quelvog, 1986). An inspection trip by the CDFG in August, 1956 noted the lake was completely full; however, their was no flow from the gate valve, which was then flushed and then operated satisfactorily at 6-1/2 turns or 1.5 second feet of flow (Lewis, 1956). Water flow in the creek prior to valve flushing was from seepage and leaks in the check dams. A subsequent inspection trip by the CDFG in August, 1958 noted the lake was 6 inches below the check dam crest and that the valve was set to release 1.4 cubic feet per second or 4-1/2 inches over the crest of the weir (Wilson, 1958)

### Quick Facts

| | |
|---|---|
| Date Constructed: | 1931 |
| Constructed By: | Leighton & Others |
| Check Dam Type: | Streamflow Maintenance |
| Check Dams: | 8 |
| Valve System: | Gate Valve/8" pipe |
| 1935 Valve Setting: | 7 turns (80 miners in) |
| 1949 Valve Setting: | 4 or 6 turns |
| Water flow Weir: | None Known |
| Lake Size: | 67 Acres |
| Drainage: | Buck Meadow Creek |
| Elevation: | 8,696 Feet |
| Date Repaired: | 1955, 1970, 1981 |

Long Lake main check dam in summer 2005 with gate valve in protected rock valve well.

| Dam | Date | Type | Length (ft) | Height (ft) | | Width (ft) | |
|---|---|---|---|---|---|---|---|
| | | | | Upstream | Downstream | Top | Base |
| Total | As Constructed | Main | 27-1/2 | 8 | 8 | 2-1/2 | 8 |
| 1 | | Main | 27 | 4.7 | 7 | 4 | 9 |
| 2 | | Saddle | 22.5 | 3.3 | 3.5 | 4.5 | 4.5 |
| 3 | | | 17.5 | 4 | 4 | 4.5 | 4.5 |
| 4 | 7/30/2005 | | 35 | 6 | 5.5 | 5 | 5 |
| 5 | | | 11.5 | 2 | 2 | 1.7 | 1.7 |
| 6 | | | 6 | 2 | 2 | 1.5 | 1.5 |
| 7 | | | 7 | 2 | 2.5 | 1 | 1 |
| 8 | | | 9 | 2 | 2 | 2.5 | 2.5 |

Check dams at Long Lake as of 2005, are generally in good condition, except for the gate valve. Much of the threaded valve stem has rusted away preventing proper operation. In addition, slight leakage is present through the main check dam. A water flow measurement weir was not present during a 2005 inspection trip.

Water was observed flowing over the crest of the main dam during the visit. In addition, a large school of trout was observed in the stream pool below the main dam. Future maintenance activities should consist of valve replacement, rock replacement along the top of the valve well, remortaring of rock, and removal of a few log snags.

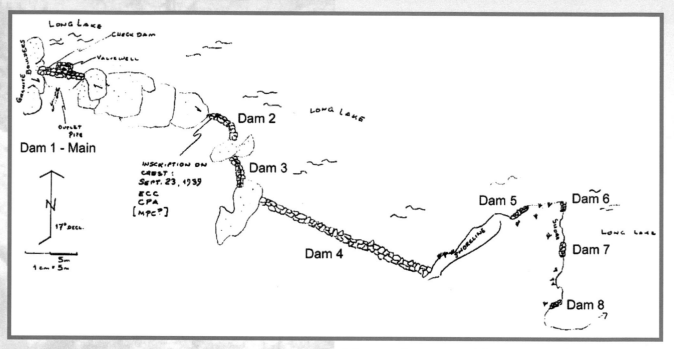

Long Lake Check Dams Sketch (Modified from and courtesy of Conners, 1986).

Check dam #2 in summer 2005 with the picturesque Long Lake in background.

School of trout below Long Lake check dam outlet stream in summer 2005.

Long Lake main, valved check dam in summer 2005. A stone and mortar valve well protects the 8 inch gate valve and wheel.

Photograph labeled as a washout at Long Lake check dam, date 10/4/1938 (Courtesy of the Tuolumne County Historical Society). This photograph may have been mislabeled, including the date, as it may depict the location of the check dam before construction in 1931.

Long Lake main check dam during construction (9/20/1931). Note the lack of a protective valve well and original valve style (Courtesy of the Tuolumne County Historical Society).

Long Lake saddle check dam #2 in 1935 with Fred Leighton on horseback (Courtesy of USDA Forest Service, Stanislaus National Forest).

Long Lake main check dam in 1935, three of the men standing in the photograph appear to be wearing Forest Service uniforms of the time (Courtesy of the USDA Forest Service, Stanislaus National Forest). Lower man is standing over outlet pipe. Photograph by Louis Jensen of Sonora.

Long Lake main check dam during construction in 1931 Note at least two highlines used for bringing rock to the work site and original pipe stem gate valve (Courtesy of the USDA Forest Service, Stanislaus National Forest).

Long Lake construction camp and crew in 1931 (Courtesy of the USDA Forest Service, Stanislaus National Forest).

Stream flow measurement weir below Long Lake main check dam in 1960. This weir was not observed during a summer 2005 inspection (Courtesy of the USDA Forest Service, Stanislaus National Forest).

# BIGELOW LAKE

A series of check dams was first constructed at Bigelow Lake in 1931 by Leighton and a work crew headed by Frank Moyle. Tom Dahl, a Sonora resident, was also a member of the work crew. The 1931 construction season resulted in the rock and mortar main dam and an earthen embankment to the northeast. This original configuration of the main check dam can be seen by the carefully fitted and hewn rocks in the lower half of the check dam. The original main check dam was constructed of tightly fitted rocks with a central rock valve pillar. In 1934, the northeast earth fill saddle check dam that was previously leaking water was replaced with a rock and mortar saddle check dam (Leighton, 1950). In 1953, a new saddle dam was constructed southwest of the main check dam due to the low-lying topography in that area and in 1954; the main check dam was raised by 3 feet, as evidenced by the difference in rock fitting and placement. In addition, a small water flow weir was constructed below the gate valve sometime after the original construction. In all, one main, valved check dam and four saddle check dams were constructed. The discrepancy in the number of saddle check dams in the historical literature may arise from several of the saddle check dams being very short and possibly having been considered one check dam in the initial count. An additional raising of the main dam may also have occurred, presumably before 1953.

In 1958, a weir insert was replaced and in 1964, the spillway section was lowered 1-1/2 feet by the California Department of Fish & Game (CDFG) at the request of the California Division of Dam Safety (Quelvog, 1986). An inspection trip by the CDFG in August, 1956 observed that water was flowing over the check dam, that the water flow measurement weir was damaged, and that recent construction work appeared to be satisfactory; however, a few minor leaks were present (Lewis, 1956). The gate valve was flushed out and adjusted so that 5 inches of water was passing over the weir or about 2.5 second feet (Lewis, 1956). A subsequent inspection trip by the CDFG in August, 1958 observed the lake level was 14 inches below the check dam crest with the dam structure in fair condition (Wilson, 1958).

### Quick Facts

Date Constructed: 1931
Constructed By    Leighton & Others
Check Dam Type:    Streamflow
Check Dams:    5
Valve System:    Gate Valve/8" Pipe
1935 Valve Setting:    4 turns
1949 Valve Setting:    3-1/2 turns
Waterflow Weir:    Yes, 3 foot wide
Lake Size:    50 Acres
Drainage:  East Fork of Cherry Creek
Elevation:    9,591 feet
Date Repaired:    1953-54, 58, 64, 70

Bigelow Lake main check dam in summer 2004. Low lake level results in minimal leakage through dam.

| Dam | Date | Type | Length (ft) | Height (ft) | | Width (ft) | |
|-----|------|------|-------------|-------------|------------|-----------|-----|
| | | | | Upstream | Downstream | Top | Base |
| Total | As Constructed | --- | 85 | 9-1/2 | 16-1/2 | 2 | 13 |
| 1 | | Saddle | 130 | 5 | 4.5 | 2.5 | 2.5 |
| 2 | | | 16 | 2 | 1 | 2 | 2 |
| 3 | 10/11/2004 | Main | 81 | --- | --- | 2.8 | --- |
| 4 | | Saddle | 14.5 | 1 | 1 | 1.5 | 1.5 |
| 5 | | | 73 | 4 | 5 | 2.8 | 2.8 |

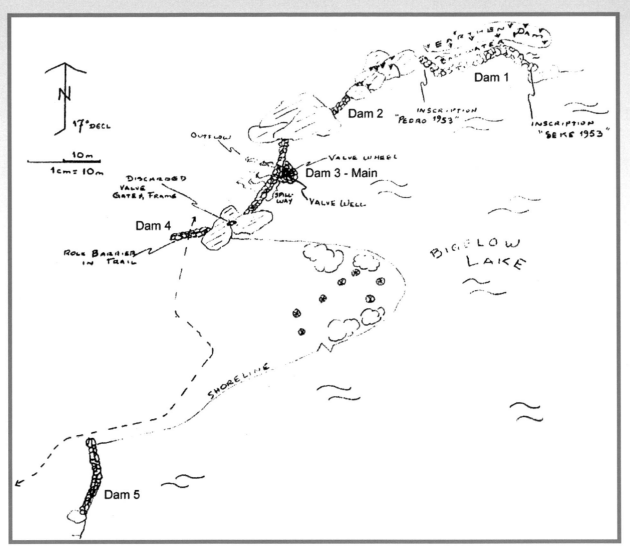

Bigelow Lake Check Dams Sketch (Modified from and courtesy of Conners, 1986).

Check dam site at Bigelow Lake before construction of original check dam in 1931
(Courtesy of the Tuolumne County Historical Society).

Bigelow Lake main check dam original configuration before 1954 reconstruction that added height, changed valve, and added a protective rock valve well to the upstream side of the check dam (Courtesy of the Tuolumne County Historical Society).

Bigelow Peak ridgeline and Bigelow Lake below in 1934 (Courtesy of Tom Dahl).

Gate valve replaced in a previous reconstruction of the main check dam (2004).

An inspection trip in 2004, observed the check dams at Bigelow Lake in fair to poor condition. Extensive leakage is present within the main check dam and is not completely evident in the current photographs due to the low lake level. In addition, extensive spalling and deterioration of the rock mortar is present. Future maintenance will likely be needed for valve replacement and rock remortaring to prevent further deterioration of these check dams.

Western rock and mortar check dam added in 1934 to replace dirt fill saddle dam at left of new check dam (10/2004).

Main check dam with protective valve well near dam center and added dam "wing" in the foreground due to adding height in 1954.

Waterflow measurement weir below main, valved check dam (10/2004).

Bigelow Lake main check dam (8/1972) with moderate lake level and minimal dam leakage (Courtesy of Brian Quelvog).

Bigelow Lake main check dam (7/1985) with normal summer time lake level and moderate leakage near internal interface between original constructed height and added height (Courtesy of Brian Quelvog).

Bigelow Lake saddle dam (7/1984) with generally normal lake level for mid summer and moderate leakage present (Courtesy of Brian Quelvog).

# EMIGRANT MEADOW LAKE

Check dams at Emigrant Meadow Lake were constructed in 1931 by Leighton and a work crew headed by Frank Moyle as a streamflow maintenance dam on the North Fork of Cherry Creek. A total of one main, valved check dam and four saddle check dams were built. It is unusual that the southernmost saddle check dam is an earth-fill dam with only a line of rocks on each side. An inspection trip in 2005 found the check dams in generally good condition, except for a broken valve handle and washed out water flow measurement weir.

**Quick Facts**

| | |
|---|---|
| Date Constructed: | 1931 |
| Constructed By: | Leighton & Others |
| Check Dam Type: | Streamflow Maintenance |
| Check Dams: | 5 |
| Valve System: | Gate Valve/8" pipe |
| 1935 Valve Setting: | 4 ½ turns (40 miners in) |
| 1949 Valve Setting: | 4 turns |
| Water flow Weir: | Yes, partially missing |
| Lake Size: | 45 Acres |
| Drainage: | North Fork of Cherry Creek |
| Elevation: | 9,407 Feet |
| Date Repaired: | 1952, 1970 |

Emigrant Meadow check dams in summer 2004.

| Dam | Date | Type | Length (ft) | Height (ft) | | Width (ft) | |
|---|---|---|---|---|---|---|---|
| | | | | Upstream | Downstream | Top | Base |
| Total | As Constructed | --- | 41 | 6-1/2 | 8-1/2 | 2-1/2 | 8 |
| 1 | | Saddle | 19 | 1.8 | 2.1 | 2.5 | 2.5 |
| 2 | | Main | 40.5 | 1.9-5.7 | 1.4-6.2 | 1.9-3 | 1.9-5.5 |
| 3 | 10/16/2004 | | 11.5 | 1.5 | 1.5 | 1.6 | 1.6 |
| 4 | | Saddle | 23.6 | 3.7 | 3.8 | 2.2 | 2.2 |
| 5 | | | 26.5 | 2 | .5 | 5.2 | 5.2 |

Party at Emigrant Meadow Lake in 1935 (Courtesy of the USDA Forest Service, Stanislaus National Forest).

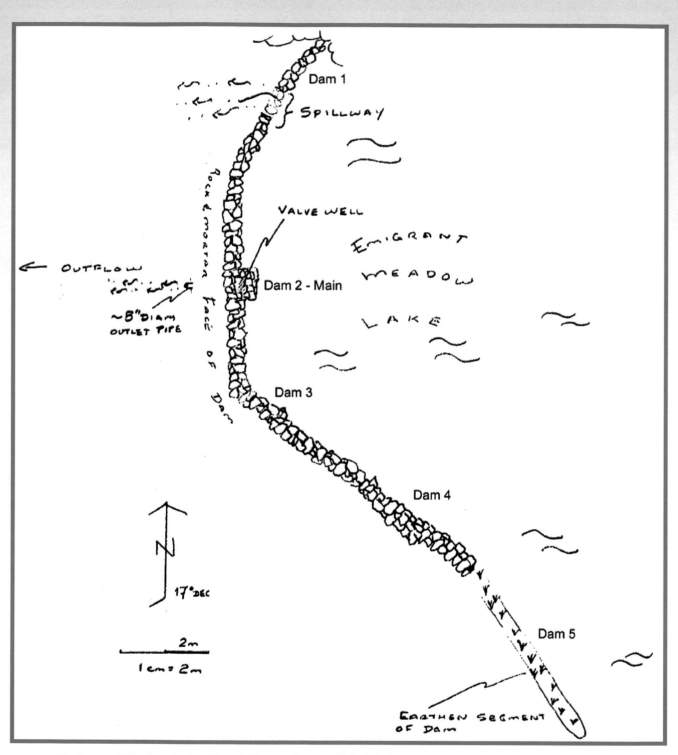

Emigrant Meadow Lake Check Dams Sketch (Modified from and courtesy of Conners, 1986).

   The check dams were reconstructed by the California Department of Fish & Game (CDFG) in 1952 (Quelvog, 1986).  An inspection trip by the CDFG in August, 1956 observed a large amount of water flowing over the check dam (Lewis, 1956).  A subsequent inspection trip by the CDFG in August, 1958 observed only a small amount of water flowing over the check dam and the dam structure was in fair condition (Wilson, 1958). The gate valve was replaced in 1987, as it was inoperable since 1970.

Emigrant Meadow Lake check dam (8/21/1950) with Emmett Stewart, Vernon Rue, and Carl Wente inspecting masonry work on the main dam. Note that valve stem is not visible near central valve pillar as shown in 1935 photographs (Courtesy of the Tuolumne County Historical Society).

Emigrant Meadow Lake check dam, date unknown; however, must be early in the year due to snow cover and water flowing over the check dam. Note that valve stem is not visible near the central valve pillar as shown in 1935 photographs (Courtesy of the Tuolumne County Historical Society).

Emigrant Meadow Lake main check dam with central valve pillar containing scribed names in mortar. Several dozen fish were observed in the stream below the check dam in October, 2004.

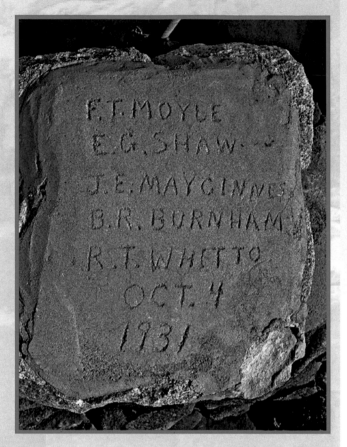

Stone valve pillar with inscribed names of workers (F. T. Moyle, E. G. Shaw, J. E. Mayginnes, B. R. Burnham, and R. T. Whitto), dated October 4, 1931.

Lake side view of stone valve pillar showing early style pipe stemmed valve in October, 2004

Possible remains of a washed out water flow measurement weir below the main check dam and gate valve outlet in October, 2004.

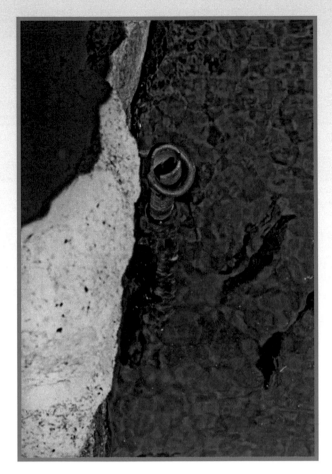

Emigrant Meadow valve stem showing extensive rust damage, 4/1985 (Courtesy of Brian Quelvog)

Emigrant Meadow valve stem after replacement, 8/1987 (Courtesy of Brian Quelvog).

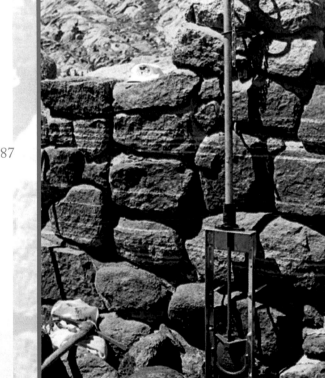

# LOWER BUCK LAKE

A single check dam at the outlet of Lower Buck Lake was constructed in 1931 by Leighton and a work crew headed by Geo Connally as a streamflow maintenance check dam on Buck Meadow Creek. Streamflow from Lower Buck Lake supports an important fishery in Wood Lake below.

The dam was reconstructed in 1953-4, an instruction plate was added, the valve stem was shortened, and logs were removed in 1968 to 1970, and mortar was replaced in 1974 by the California Department of Fish & Game (CDFG). An inspection trip by the CDFG in August, 1956 observed that water was flowing over the check dam and that the valve grills was plugged, not allowing water to pass (Lewis, 1956). Leighton, on an inspection trip the year before on October 31, noted no flow in Louse Canyon. A subsequent inspection trip by the CDFG in August, 1958 again observed water flowing over the top of the check dam and the dam structure was in good condition (Wilson, 1958).

Lower Buck Lake check dam
in summer 1990.

**Quick Facts**

| | |
|---|---|
| Date Constructed: | 1931 |
| Constructed By: | Leighton & Others |
| Check Dam Type: | Streamflow |
| Check Dams: | 1 |
| Valve System: | Gate Valve/8" pipe |
| 1935 Valve Setting: | 4 turns (6 mnr in) |
| Water flow Weir: | None Found |
| Lake Size: | 40 Acres |
| Drainage: | Buck Meadow Creek |
| Elevation: | 8,305 Feet |
| Date Repaired: | 1954, 1968-70, 1974, 1981 |

| Dam | Date | Type | Length (ft) | Height (ft) | | Width (ft) | |
|---|---|---|---|---|---|---|---|
| | | | | Upstream | Downstream | Top | Base |
| Total | As Constructed | --- | 41 | 8 | 12 | 3 | 10 |
| 1 | 10/14/2004 | Main | 44.3 | 4.0-5.5 | 8.5 | 4.5 | 6 |

Lower Buck Lake check dam in 1935 with five logs on dam crest (Courtesy of the USDA Forest Service, Stanislaus National Forest).

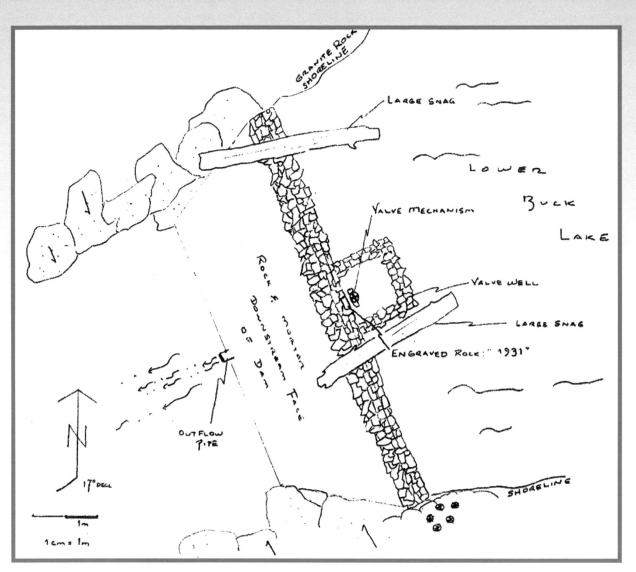

Lower Buck Lake Check Dam Sketch (Modified from and courtesy of Conners, 1986).

Lower Buck Lake check dam in July, 2005 with large upstream log jam and logs wedged across crest and lower face of check dam. Extensive water flow was also present as apparent in this mid-summer photograph.

Fred Leighton looking for a check dam site in August 1930 at Lower Buck Lake (Leighton Collection Photograph, Courtesy of Bruce DeMott).

Buck Lake check dam (7/22/1935) before reconstruction in 1935 that added a new valve and protective valve well (Courtesy of the Tuolumne County Historical Society).

Chiseled "1931" boulder in rock protective valve well (10/2004). This rock must have originally been placed within the valve pillar that is evident in the photograph to left and when the check dam was reconstructed, was added to the new valve well in this rotated view (note valve stem and handle).

Inspection trips in 2004 and 2005 found the single check dam at Lower Buck Lake in fair to poor condition. Several log snags are present on the check dam along with minor leakage within the dam. Several large log jams are also present in the lake above the check dam. Extensive rust damage is present on the valve stem that may prevent proper operation. In addition, a water flow measurement weir was not present. Future maintenance activities will likely consist of valve replacement, removal of log snags, and rock remortaring.

Lower Buck Lake check dam (8/1984) during CDFG inspection. Minimal log debris on dam compared to other years (Courtesy of Brian Quelvog).

Lower Buck Lake from check dam (4/1985). Valve well in foreground and numerous logs and debris along the shoreline (Courtesy of Brian Quelvog).

Lower Buck Lake looking upstream from check dam (4/1985). Log jam present in foreground area of lake (Courtesy of Brian Quelvog).

# EMIGRANT LAKE

In 1931, Leighton and a work crew headed by Frank Moyle constructed check dams at Emigrant Lake. These check dams were intended to maintain streamflow on the North Fork of Cherry Creek. One major main, valved check dam and one short saddle check dam were constructed. In 1934, the main check dam was raised 2 feet.

The California Department of Fish & Game (CDFG) reconstructed the check dam in 1952. Quelvog notes the water flow measurement weir below the dam was broken in 1964 (Quelvog, 1986); however, field inspection in the summer of 2004 failed to discover the remains of this weir structure. Inspection trips by the CDFG in August 1956 and 1958 observed water flowing over the top of the dam in both years and in 1958, flow over the weir was about 9-1/2 cubic feet per second (Lewis, 1956; Wilson, 1958).

Panoramic view of Emigrant Lake main check dam in summer 2004 with both outlet pipes visible in outlet stream. Main check dam is severely damaged in central portion as at least three rock courses are missing and adjacent stones are held in place with loose mortar.

## Quick Facts

| | | | |
|---|---|---|---|
| Date Constructed: | 1931 | Water flow Weir: | None observed |
| Constructed By: | Leighton and Others | Lake Size: | 195 Acres |
| Check Dam Type: | Streamflow Maintenance | Drainage: | North Fork of Cherry Creek |
| Check Dams: | 2 | Elevation: | 8,827 Feet |
| Valve System: | Gate Valve and 8" pipes | Date Repaired: | 1934, 1952, 1970 |
| 1935 Valve Setting: | Pipe open and valve at 6 turns (200 miners inches) | | |

| Dam | Date | Type | Length (ft) | Height (ft) | | Width (ft) | |
|---|---|---|---|---|---|---|---|
| | | | | Upstream | Downstream | Top | Base |
| Total | As Constructed | --- | 35 | 9 | 9 | 2-1/2 | 8 |
| 1 | 10/15/2004 | Main | 57.6 | 1.1-3.4 | 0.6-6.6 | 1.8-2.7 | 1.9-7 |
| 2 | | Saddle | 10.2 | 2.1 | 1.8 | 2.6 | 2.6 |

An inspection trip in 2004 observed significant deterioration of the main check dam and a very poor overall condition. A significant breached area along with tension cracks in the rock mortar is present as shown in the photograph above. This area appears to have failed into the dam to the interface of a previous dam height addition. Deterioration of this area of the main check dam started earlier than 1993, as evidenced by extensive leakage in a photograph below taken during a previous State check dam inspection. A gate valve was not present during the inspection; however, two 8 inch outlet pipes were visible on the downstream side of the main check dam. Much of the area where a gate valve should exist is obscured by a log snag and other debris. In addition, a water flow measurement weir was not present.

Future maintenance activities should consist of repair of the partially breached area, rock remortaring of the entire main check dam, gate valve replacement, and removal of log snags and other debris.

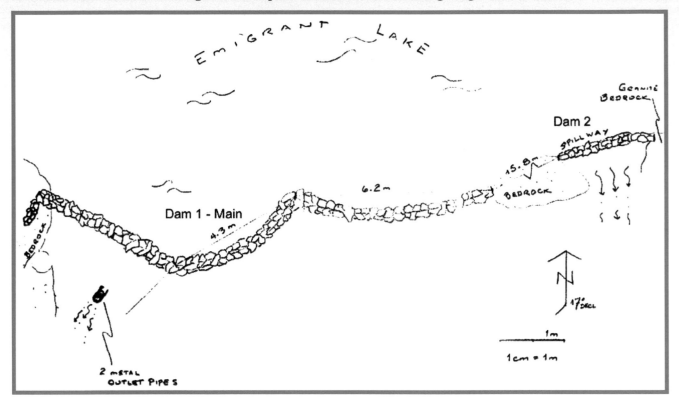

Emigrant Lake Check Dams Sketch (Modified from and courtesy of Conners, 1986).

Emigrant Lake main check dam (labeled as 1935; however, the main check dam was raised 2 feet in 1934 and this photograph appears to represent near-original configuration). A valve well appears to be present at the left end of the check dam above the outlet pipes (Courtesy of the USDA Forest Service, Stanislaus National Forest).

Fred Leighton, Karl DeFiebre, Dick Kronke, and Louie Fraguero at Emigrant Lake in 1938 (Leighton Collection Photograph, Courtesy of Bruce DeMott).

Emigrant Lake main check dam in 1960 showing characteristic "S" shape and unbreached section (Courtesy of the USDA Forest Service, Stanislaus National Forest).

Emigrant Lake main check dam (8/1984) with Bob Marshall, Jake Parsons, and Harry Weston. Check dam is generally in good condition, note interface between original height and added height (Courtesy of Brian Quelvog).

Emigrant Lake spillway or saddle check dam (4/1985) with water flow over the spillway (Courtesy of Brian Quelvog).

Emigrant Lake main check dam (9/3/1993) during Division of Safety of Dams inspection showing significant leaks. Dam crest above shows significant cracking in other related photographs. Area will eventually breach as shown in lower photograph (Persson, 1993).

Emigrant Lake main check dam (10/2004) showing breached upper portion of check dam, most likely within that portion of check dam added in 1934.

# THE U. S. FOREST SERVICE AND THE CIVILIAN CONSERVATION CORPS GETS INVOLVED (1932-1941)

Leighton's success with the second phase of check dam construction resulted in continued efforts with the Tuolumne County Fish and Game Association, the California State Chamber of Commerce, U. S. Forest Service, and additionally, the Civilian Conservation Corps (CCC). This work would lead to the construction of eight check dams from 1933 to 1941 at Y-Meadow, Bear Lake, Horse Meadow, Cow Meadow Lake, Huckleberry Lake, Snow Lake, Cooper Meadow, and Whitesides Meadow. It would also be the first time a check dam was constructed with the intent to sub-irrigate mountain meadows at Horse, Cooper, and Whitesides Meadows with a new check dam type.

Leighton organized an inspection trip for 5 days with members of the Statewide Fish and Game Committee in 1932. The intent of this trip was to inspect previously constructed check dams and proposed new check dam sites in the Emigrant Basin. At a pre-trip meeting at Dardanelle Hotel on September 4, 1932, trip members gathered to discuss the check dam concept. They noted that:

> "*one dry season* [would] *wipe out all the good done by several continuous wet seasons, particularly in the streams ...[that by] maintaining continuous stream flow, the new hatch* [of fish] *will be permitted to live and serve to restock the stream and large lakes below ... estimated that 90 days protection by storage of flood waters* [would] *be ample to guarantee continuous stream flow ... and that ...fish food* [would] *also be protected and increased by the use of check dams*" (State CC, 1932).

Leighton's inspection trip started at Kennedy Meadows on September 5, 1932, to observe check dams at Emigrant Lake, Emigrant Meadow Lake, a proposed check dam site at Cow Meadows Lake, Buck Lake, and Long Lake. Members of the inspection trip included several prominent people of the time (Leighton, 1963; State CC, 1932), including:

Dr. Theodore J. Hoover, Stanford University – Committee Chairman
J. R. Hall – Stanislaus National Forest Supervisor
John Farley – Fish and Game Commission Executive Officer
Clarence Bennett- Fish and Game Sub-Commission of Central Coast CC Chairman
A. C. Steven – Canadian Bank of Commerce (San Francisco) President

Members of the inspection trip also included E. R. McAuley – Fish and Game Commission Chief of Patrol; D. W. Morrison – State Division of Water Resources Engineer; Ed Burgeson - Tuolumne County Fish and Game Association Secretary; Louis Jensen – Sonora Cameraman; Frank Kurzi - Kennedy Meadows Packer and Guide; Gordon Alexander – Assistant Packer; William Kinney – Cook; Raymond Harry – Assistant Cook; and J. A. Carey – Brightman Station Ranger.

By the time the inspection party reached the proposed dam site at Snow Lake on the second day, the members were "*well sold on the value of the check dam*" (State CC, 1932). They observed ideal trout propagation in areas of existing check dams, including several thousand 4- and 5-inch fish in the two miles upstream of Huckleberry Lake that also included fish hatched in 1932. In passing Cow Meadows, the members inspected spawning grounds and a 15-acre lake. They suggested building a 2-foot-high check dam at the outlet of the meadow because a check dam might raise water levels enough to connect the small lake with the stream and would provide increased trout propagation (State CC, 1932). Streams crossed during the trip were likely flowing as a result of previously built check dams and water was discharging from the outlets of Emigrant, Bigelow, Buck, and Long Lakes. The inspection party also observed that a check dam constructed at Snow Lake would provide stream flows to that portion of Cherry Creek above the confluence of the stream draining Bigelow Lake and a check dam constructed at Cow Meadow would provide important fish habitat and spawning areas for increased fish propagation.

The members, in a meeting at the Dardanelle Resort after the inspection trip, wrote *"it was estimated that this system of check dams will maintain stream flow in about 75 miles of stream which would otherwise go dry for a few weeks this year and every other year except where a series of wet seasons prevailed"* (State CC, 1932). Each inspection party that visited the Emigrant Basin during this time made similar conclusions as to the usefulness of the check dams to fish propagation and stream flow.

Funding for check dams at Cow Meadow, Huckleberry Lake, Horse Meadow, Snow Lake, and Emigrant Lake came from Mr. Shaw, USFS Regional Forester in $10,000 for Stream Flow Maintenance activities (Leighton, 1978).

Another inspection trip was organized by John Farley, a Division of Fish and Game Executive Officer, on September 15, 1933 into the Emigrant Basin for the purpose of inspecting the previous work from 1931 by A. E. Burghduff of the department and in promoting future check dam construction by the Civilian Conservation Corps at Bear Lake and Y-Meadow. The trip was attended by A. E. Burghduff, Fred Leighton, Bill Burnham, Bill Warne, and Ray Harry. Leighton noted that during this inspection trip, all the canyons they passed were dry.

1932 Inspection Party, Left to Right: Dean Hoover, Ed Burgeson, John Farley, E. McAuley, A. Stevens, D. Morrison, Clarance Bennett, Jess Hall, Frank Kurzi, and Fred Leighton
(Courtesy of the Tuolumne County Historical Society).

A second inspection trip was organized in 1933 (September 20-24) by Fred Tatton, the Manager of the Central Valley Council, State Chamber of Commerce, so Dr. Paul R. Needham of the U. S. Bureau of Fisheries (now the U. S. Fish and Wildlife Service), a leading fishery biologist of the time, could observe and review the check dam concept in the Emigrant Basin. The trip was attended by Fred Tatton, Dr. Needham, Fred Leighton, W. A. Perkins, and Glen Shaw. Dr. Needham noted the same low flow summer conditions that Leighton and others had observed, *"September is low-water month when many streams go completely dry, depending upon the amount of precipitation in the previous winter"* and *"such unstable conditions are most destructive to trout"* (Needham, 1934). Needham observed in the stream below Lower Buck Lake where a check dam was constructed in 1931 that *"many fine trout from three to sixteen inches in length"* were present and in the stream above Upper Buck Lake the stream *"had dried up expect for standing water in some of the deeper pools"* and that *"there was not a drop of water flowing over the riffles"* resulting in *"hundreds of young trout hatched this year in the process of being destroyed by low water"* (Needham, 1933).

After the inspection trip, Needham concluded that "*about ten miles of fine spawning grounds* [had] *been made safe breeding area ... and the thousands of trout seen ... indicate that as a practical conservation measure, the dams installed are steadily paying for themselves from year to year in adding large numbers of young trout ... in both streams and lakes*" and that "*not only are fish being saved by flow maintenance, but their food organisms as well*". While Needham was in favor of the small Emigrant Basin check dams for fish propagation and survival, he was very concerned about the construction of large dams on the Columbia and Sacramento Rivers' impact to native fish (Needham, 1947), further reinforcing Leighton's idea of conservation.

Leighton continued his check dam concept by promoting the use of Civilian Conservation Corps (CCC) work crews to construct check dams. In April 1933, Leighton enlisted help from the California State Chamber of Commerce in the use of CCC crews in building check dams. A May 1933 letter advocated the use of CCC labor by using a sub-camp of 10 to 20 men at each proposed dam site between July 15th and October (Leighton, 1933).

Jess Hall, the Stanislaus National Forest Supervisor, was not able to keep to CCC crews busy during 1933, so he asked the Tuolumne County Fish & Game Association for potential work projects. Leighton, as the Fish & Game Association President, suggested building more check dams, including those at Bear Lake and Y-Meadow (Leighton, 1972). By July, Jess Hall had arranged for the establishment of two CCC sub-camps at Bear Lake and Y-Meadow; however, regulations existing at the time required daily inspections and a phone available in the CCC camps. Due to the remote location east of Pinecrest where a main CCC camp (Strawberry Camp) had been established earlier, daily inspections and the installation of a phone were not possible. Leighton in July 1933 urged Major Farley that the regulations be changed so that work could proceed on additional check dams (Leighton, 1933). Using Leighton's idea of CCC check dam construction, John Farley of the California Department of Fish and Game wanted to extend the project to other forests in 1933 (Farley, 1933).

Construction of a check dam at Bear Lake by the CCC started in August. By late September 1933, the check dam at Bear Lake had been constructed and work was started on Y-Meadow Dam (Burghduff, 1933). A late fall snowstorm halted construction at

Y-Meadow Dam and was finished in the summer of 1934 (TCFGA, 1934).

During the summer of 1934, Y-Meadow Dam was completed and check dams at Horse Meadow, Cow Meadow, Huckleberry Lake, and Snow Lake were built by the CCC under direction from the Stanislaus National Forest. In addition, the existing check dam at Emigrant Lake was raised 2 feet and a fish ladder was constructed in Cherry Creek above Emigrant Lake. Construction proceeded with $10,000 in funds donated by the Forest Service Regional Supervisor (Leighton, 1969) using CCC labor. Because a rock ledge prevented fish from spawning above Emigrant Lake, a fish ladder was built by blasting out portions of the ledge (TCFGA, 1934).

Leighton suggested valve settings to J. R. Hall, the Stanislaus National Forest Supervisor in 1935 for gate valves at Bigelow Lake, Horse Meadow, Huckleberry Lake, Emigrant Meadow Lake, Cow Meadow Lake, Lower Buck Lake, Long Lake, Y-Meadow Dam, and Bear Lake (Leighton, 1935). The setting for the Snow Lake gate valve had not yet been determined and was omitted. No mention of how these flows were determined or measured at the check dams is available in the literature that survives to this day; however, in later years, weirs were constructed and used for stream flow measurement at several lakes, including Snow Lake, Bigelow Lake, Middle Emigrant Lake, and Emigrant Meadow Lake.

A 1939 article in the *Stockton Daily Evening Record* newspaper promoted Leighton's check dam conservation concept by highlighting the gains made during previous years proclaiming "*Cherry Creek and its tributaries are now living streams*" by "*maintaining some stream flow every day of the year*" as "*thousands of native Rainbow trout dies as a result*" of no water flow (1939). Leighton's comment on the success of the check dams at the time was "*the test has been made. It has proven the need for check dams all along the summit of the Sierra and such projects should hold high priority in conservation in California*" (1939), indicating his desire to continue the check dam project at other locations in the Sierras. Throughout Leighton's involvement in the check dam project, he stressed natural fisheries and conservation as "*every recreationist who likes lakes and running streams and who believes in natural reproduction of a bountiful supply of trout and maintenance of fish life throughout the year, all at low cost, should insist on a comprehensive survey of the existing situation and establishment of check dams where required*" (Leighton, 1939).

# Y-MEADOW DAM

Construction on the Y-Meadow check dam was begun in 1933 by the Civilian Conservation Corps (CCC); however, an early season snow storm resulted in the Stanislaus National Forest completing the check dam in the summer of 1934. Y-Meadow Dam is the only check dam that created a lake where a natural lake did not exist prior and was constructed as a lake level check dam to provide water flows within Lily Creek, past Bear Lake, and eventually into the Clavey River. The dam top crest narrows significantly at the western end for an unknown reason.

On August 8, 1950 Leighton took a diver, who was also his mechanic from Sonora, to the dam site so that a stuck valve could be opened and the lake gradually drained (Leighton, 1950). Leighton had observed the valve was inoperable the year before during an inspection trip with H. O. Pruitt. On September 5, 1950, Leighton made a second trip to the check dam to replace the valve stem that had broken about 12 feet below the dam crest. He intended to use a solid steel rod instead of the pipe that had been used earlier. Because Leighton surmised that the original valve stem had been damaged from ice and freezing, he suggested that the new valve be placed on the downstream side (Leighton, 1950). This outlet pipe was not observed in summer 2004 and may be covered by additional rock fill or simply rusted back under the check dam. An inspection trip by the CDFG in August, 1956 observed that the lake level was 3 feet from the top of the check dam and that the gate valve was not functioning correctly (Lewis, 1956). An inspection trip in 2004 observed the check dam in good condition, except for a missing gate valve stem handle. Future maintenance activities should consist of rock remortaring and gate valve replacement.

Panoramic view of Y-Meadow check dam in summer 2004.

## Quick Facts

| | | | |
|---|---|---|---|
| Date Constructed: | 1933-1934 | 1935 Valve Setting: | 3 ½ turns (25 miners in) |
| Constructed By: | CCC & USFS | Water flow Weir: | None Found |
| Check Dam Type: | Lake Level | Lake Size: | 20 Acres |
| Check Dams: | 1 | Drainage: | Lily Creek, Clavey River |
| Valve System: | Gate Valve/8" pipe (Missing - 2004) | Elevation: | |
| | 8,500 Feet | Date Repaired: | 1950, 1964 |

| Dam | Date | Type | Length (ft) | Height (ft) | | Width (ft) | |
|---|---|---|---|---|---|---|---|
| | | | | Upstream | Downstream | Top | Base |
| Total | As Constructed | --- | 84 | 24 | 26 | 4 | 30 |
| 1 | 7/4/2004 | Main | 89.2 | 15.8 | 26.0 | 1.5 – 3.5 | 23.4 |

Y-Meadow check dam (1934) during construction (Courtesy of the Tuolumne County Historical Society). Note use of high lines to transport rock to the work site.

Y-Meadow check dam (1934) during construction (Courtesy of the Tuolumne County Historical Society).

Y-Meadow check dam site (1933). Two men are visible on granite outcrop to right of stream; one is holding a rod (Courtesy of the USDA Forest Service, Stanislaus National Forest).

Painted survey stationing used during construction of the Y-Meadow check dam (7/2004).

Y-Meadow check dam (7/2004).

Wire rope cable and steel rock anchor used during construction of the Y-Meadow check dam (7/2004). May have been used with overhead high line structures to help move large rocks into position within the check dam.

# BEAR LAKE

A check dam was constructed at Bear Lake in 1933 by the Civilian Conservation Corps (CCC) as a streamflow maintenance dam on Lily Creek which eventually flows into the Clavey River. The single check dam at the lake outlet has deteriorated significantly since it was built and the gate valve is no longer present; however, the valve itself may be obscured by a partial log jam and the valve stem is known to be missing.

As early as 1984, it was noted from inspection trips that leaks were present and in 1985, the cap of the dam was missing in several locations (Quelvog, 1986). The gate valve is longer present, at least one rock course of the dam has broken away, and significant portions of the downstream benches of the check dam are missing. An inspection trip by the CDFG in August, 1956 observed the lake level was 8 inches from the top of the check dam and that the gate valve was rusted (Lewis, 1956). While on this trip, Leighton suggested building the check dam higher an additional 12 inches to help prevent log damage and to construct a fish ladder "*which would allow fish to migrate for spawning*" (Lewis, 1956).

Bear Lake check dam (1933) during construction (Courtesy of the Tuolumne County Historical Society).

## Quick Facts

| | | | |
|---|---|---|---|
| Date Constructed: | 1933 | 1949 Valve Setting | 5 turns |
| Constructed By: | Leighton & Others | Water flow Weir: | None Found |
| Check Dam Type: | Streamflow Maintenance | Lake Size: | 24 Acres |
| Check Dams: | 1 | Drainage: | Lily Creek, Clavey River |
| Valve System: | Gate Valve/8" pipe (2004: Missing) | Elevation: | 7,691 Feet |
| 1935 Valve Setting: | 5 ½ turns (50 miners in) | Date Repaired: | Unknown |

| Dam | Date | Type | Length (ft) | Height (ft) | | Width (ft) | |
|---|---|---|---|---|---|---|---|
| | | | | Upstream | Downstream | Top | Base |
| Total | As Constructed | --- | 50 | 10 | 12 | 3 | 12 |
| 1 | 7/5/2004 | Main | 51.0 | --- | ~ 6 | 3 – 6 | --- |

The check dam at Bear Lake is in very poor condition, as observed in a 2004 inspection trip. Several rock courses and the gate valve are completely missing. Significant deterioration of rock mortar was also observed. The growth of brush has obscured the outlet and much of the lower rock courses of the check dam. Several log snags are also present in the lake behind the check dam, on the dam crest, and in the stream below. No water flow measurement weir was present. Future maintenance activities will likely consist of rock replacement in several rock courses, remortaring, and replacement of the gate valve.

Bear Lake check dam (1933) during construction (Courtesy of the Tuolumne County Historical Society).

Bear Lake check dam (1933) during construction, Louie Folletti – Foreman at left (Courtesy of the Tuolumne County Historical Society).

Bear Lake check dam in July, 1985 showing signs of deterioration (Courtesy of Brian Quelvog).

Bear Lake check dam in July, 1997 showing additional deterioration
(Courtesy of Brian Quelvog).

Bear Lake check dam (7/2004). Note severely deteriorated rock
courses and missing gate valve.

# HORSE MEADOW

A single check dam at Horse Meadow was constructed in 1934 by the Civilian Conservation Corps (CCC) to sub-irrigate the meadow for grazing and meadow enhancement.

In 1960 the check dam was reconstructed by the Stanislaus National Forest. An inspection trip by the California Department of Fish and Game (CDFG) in August, 1958 observed that "*18 to 24 inches of the crest had broken off*" and "*that the water table in the meadow was down to 16 inches*" (Wilson, 1958). An inspection trip by the CDFG in 1984 observed that approximately 18 inches of the crest were missing again and that sediment was within 12 inches of the crest (Quelvog, 1986). Quelvog recommended at that time adding a gate valve and notes that no gate valve was present as early as 1958, indicating the original gate valve disappeared sometime between construction in 1934 and 1958.

Panoramic view of Horse Meadow check dam in August, 2004. Much of the check dam has been broken apart by the elements, and the gate valve stem and handle is missing. Eight-inch outlet pipe visible in lower center of photograph, partially obscured.

| Dam | Date | Type | Length (ft) | Height (ft) | | Width (ft) | |
|---|---|---|---|---|---|---|---|
| | | | | Upstream | Downstream | Top | Base |
| Total | As Constructed | --- | ? | ? | 8 | 2 | ? |
| 1 | 10/12/2004 | Main | 52.0 | 2.0 | 5.0 | 4.6 – 5.6 | 4.6 – 5.6 |

In a study commissioned by the SNF in 1988, it was determined that that due to the sloping nature of Horse Meadow, it was unlikely that the check dam had a significant effect on ground water levels within the meadow (deGraff, 1988); however, photographs from 1935 and 1950 (shown below) indicates a partially flooded meadow that probably would not have occurred without the check dam. In addition, the study assumed the meadow sloped significantly, which has not been verified to this day by surveying. Historical photographs clearly detail a partially to moderately flooded meadow which indicates that initially the check dam at Horse Meadow did in fact provide water storage and meadow irrigation. This was significantly reduced as the check dam fell into disrepair and today probably provides no significant increase to ground water levels within Horse Meadow, other than to prevent upward erosion of the East Fork of Cherry Creek.

A field inspection in 2004 observed the check dam at Horse Meadow in very poor condition. Much of the check dam has deteriorated to the point that it probably no longer raises water levels within Horse Meadow. In addition, the gate valve is completely missing; however, the outlet pipe is obscured by rock debris. Future maintenance activities should include rock replacement, remortaring, and valve replacement.

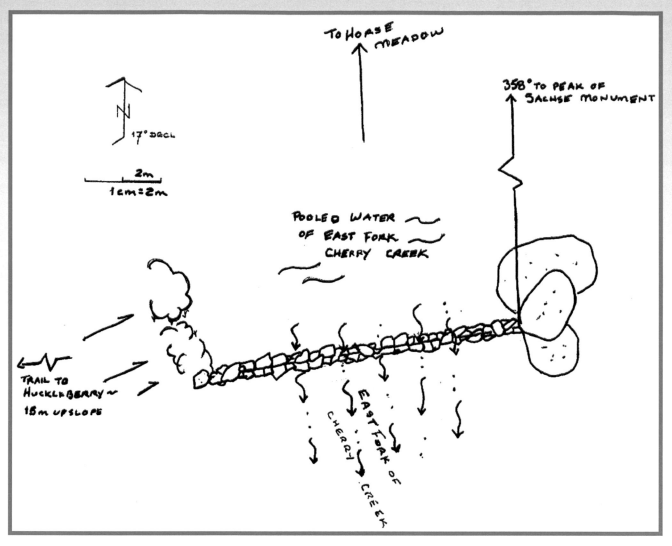

Horse Meadow Check Dam Sketch (Modified from and courtesy of Conners, 1986).

Partially flooded Horse Meadow (8/10/1935) after construction of a check dam in 1934 (Courtesy of the USDA Forest Service, Stanislaus National Forest).

View of Horse Meadow (1934) from east near site of check dam, possibly before check dam construction (Courtesy of Tom Dahl).

Paul Castle, Larry Fraguero, Allan Miller, Carl Wente, W. E. Stewart, and Vernon Ruc overlooking Horse Meadow on August 21, 1950. Meandering East Fork of Cherry Creek within Horse Meadow with flooded oxbow bends shown (Leighton Collection Photograph, Courtesy of Bruce DeMott).

Eastern end of Horse Meadow on August 21, 1950 with flooded oxbow bends of the East Fork of Cherry Creek and other ponds. Photographer's fingers probably are evident at left side of photograph (Leighton Collection Photograph, Courtesy of Bruce DeMott).

Horse Meadow check dam in 1960, possibly after reconstruction (Courtesy of the USDA Forest Service, Stanislaus National Forest).

Horse Meadow check dam in 1960 during inspection, possibly after reconstruction (Courtesy of the USDA Forest Service, Stanislaus National Forest).

Horse Meadow check dam in October, 1984 showing several rock courses missing and no gate valve (Courtesy of Brian Quelvog).

# COW MEADOW LAKE

Check dams at Cow Meadow Lake were constructed in 1934 by the Stanislaus National Forest and the Civilian Conservation Corps as a lake level dam. Rocks were transported to the check dam construction site using a highline and wooden platform from the talus slope to the south.

The check dams were repaired in 1966 and in 1980 by the California Department of Fish and Game (CDFG). An inspection trip by the CDFG in August, 1956 observed the main check dam was in very bad condition due to "*high water with logs and debris*" with only 25 to 30 percent remaining. In addition, the CDFG recommended the dam be rebuilt in 1957 and additional reinforcement be used (Lewis, 1956) in re-building the check dam. This was the last dam that Andy Weaver, the CDFG hatchery supervisor, was involved in and marked the end of hatchery involvement in the check dams.

**Quick Facts**

| | |
|---|---:|
| Date Constructed: | 1931 |
| Constructed By: | USFS/CCC |
| Check Dam Type: | Lake Level |
| Number of Dams: | 4 |
| Valve System: | None |
| 1935 Valve Setting: | Plug pipe |
| Lake Size: | 60 Acres |
| Drainage: | N Fork of Cherry Creek |
| Elevation: | 7,780 feet |
| Date Repaired: | 1980 |

Main Cow Meadow check dam (1968) before washout (Courtesy of the USDA Forest Service, Stanislaus National Forest).

| Dam | Date | Type | Length (ft) | Height (ft) | | Width (ft) | |
|---|---|---|---|---|---|---|---|
| | | | | Upstream | Downstream | Top | Base |
| Total | As Constructed | --- | 91.5 (#4) | ? | ? | 2 | ? |
| 1 | | | 20 | 3.7 | 2.3 | 2.5 | 2.5 |
| 2 | 8/3/2005 | Saddle | 19 | 3 | 3.5 | 1.7 | 1.7 |
| 3 | | | --- | --- | --- | --- | --- |
| 4 | | Main | Dam now washed out. | | | | |

An inspection trip in 2005 found the Cow Meadow Lake main check dam completely washed out and the three saddle check dams in good condition. Numerous holes drilled into the granite bedrock in an attempt to anchor the previous check dam are visible in the streambed. Prior to washout of the main check dam, several log snags were cabled off in the lake above to prevent them from lodging against the check dam. It has been reported that at least one cable showed evidence of being cut soon after the main check dam washed out. If these cables had been intentionally cut, the log snags would have floated down stream and struck the low check dam, possibly creating a massive breach.

Future maintenance activities would require complete replacement of the main check dam and rock remortaring of the saddle check dams. As all of the individual rocks of the main check dam have washed downstream, additional rock collecting will be required for replacement of the check dam. A likely source of rock would be the talus slope to the south of the lake outlet, an area used as a source of rock for the original check dams.

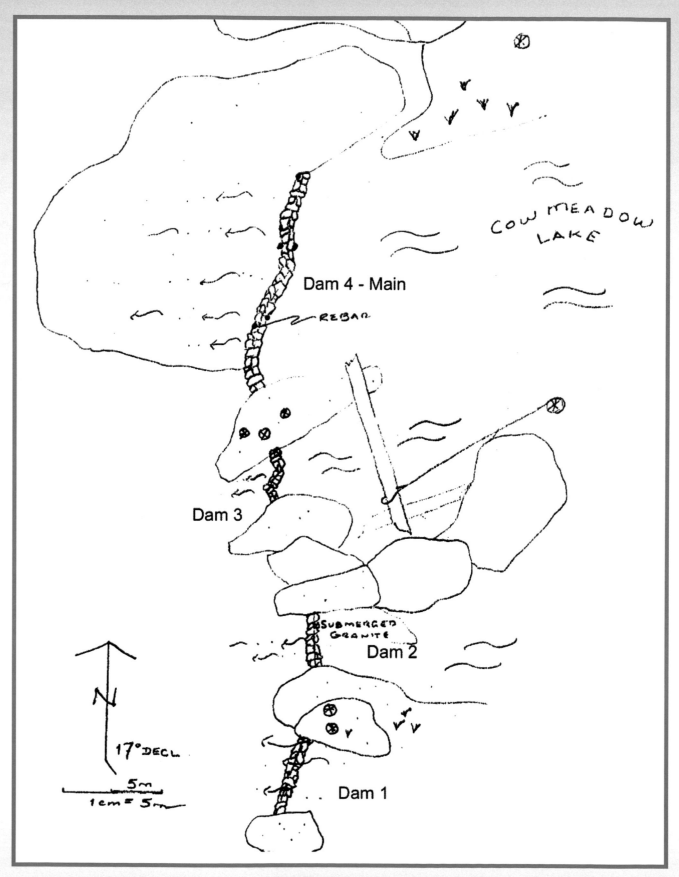

Dam 4 - Main

REBAR

COW MEADOW LAKE

Dam 3

SUBMERGED GRANITE

Dam 2

N

17° DECL

5m

1cm = 5m

Dam 1

Cow Meadow Check Dams Sketch (Modified from and courtesy of Conners, 1986).

Cow Meadow Lake check dam construction, date unknown – sometime in 1934. Cable line used for transporting rock to the work site (Courtesy of the Tuolumne County Historical Society).

Cow Meadow Lake check dam construction, date unknown – sometime in 1934. Cable line used for transporting rock to the work site (Courtesy of the Tuolumne County Historical Society).

Cow Meadow Lake main check dam location (8/2005). Check dam washed out earlier.

Cow Meadow main check dam in August, 1993 with breach from log jam (Courtesy of Brian Quelvog).

Cow Meadow main check dam in August, 1993 with breach from log jam (Courtesy of Brian Quelvog).

Cow Meadow Lake saddle check dam (8/2005).

Picturesque Cow Meadow Lake near check dam (8/2005).

Cow Meadow saddle check dam in August, 1990 (Courtesy of Brian Quelvog).

Cow Meadow main check dam in August, 1989 before washout (Courtesy of Brian Quelvog).

# HUCKLEBERRY LAKE

Check dams at Huckleberry Lake were constructed in 1934 by the Civilian Conservation Corps. One main, valved dam and 10 saddle dams were built between granite boulders and rock outcrops at the outlet of the lake due to the broad, open outlet area.

In 1956, the California Department of Fish and Game (CDFG) inspected the check dams and found most of the check dams in good condition, but did recommend that two small, deteriorating saddle dams be repaired the next year by adding 6 inches in height (Lewis, 1956). One of the saddle dams (east) was rebuilt in September, 1971 by Laird Marshall (Moccasin Hatchery Superintendent), Fred Cavagnaro (Moccasin Hatchery Assistant), Fred M., Willi Ritts, and Jay Gilbert (Kennedy Meadows Resort), Vince Dona (CDFG Warden), Jack Kay, Jerry Warder, and Bob Devine (sportsman) with funding from the CDFG and Tuolumne County (Leighton, 1971).

### Quick Facts

| | |
|---|---|
| Date Constructed: | 1934 |
| Constructed By: | CCC |
| Check Dam Type: | Streamflow |
| Number of Dams: | 11 |
| Valve System: | Gate Valve/8" pipe |

1935 Valve Setting: Keep closed, except in dry season.

| | |
|---|---|
| Lake Size: | 133 Acres |
| Drainage: | East Fork of Cherry Creek |
| Elevation: | 8,827 feet |
| Date Repaired: | 1971 |

Huckleberry Lake main check dam with intact and working gate valve and outlet (10/2004).

| Dam | Date | Type | Length (ft) | Height (ft) | | Width (ft) | |
|---|---|---|---|---|---|---|---|
| | | | | Upstream | Downstream | Top | Base |
| Total | As Constructed | --- | 92 | 3 | 3 | 2 | 3 |
| 1 | | | 16.0 | 1.0 | 1.2 | 2.9 | 2.9 |
| 2 | | | 45.1 | 1.9 | 1.7 | 1.5 | 1.5 |
| 3 | | | 18 | 1.4 | 2.0 | 1.5 | 1.5 |
| 4 | | Saddle | 7.2 | 1.9 | 1.6 | 1.7 | 1.7 |
| 5 | | | 3.0 | Obscured | 1.0 | 1.7 | 1.7 |
| 6 | 10/13/2004 | | 21.5 | 1.6 | 1.6 | 2.7 | 2.7 |
| 7 | | | 7.8 | 1.7 | 2.9 | 1.4 | 1.4 |
| 8 | | | 11.0 | 1.2 | 2.3 | 1.3 | 1.3 |
| 9 | | Main | 11.0 | 2.4 | 3.5 | 2.2 | 2.2 |
| 10 | | Saddle | 9.0 | 2.0 | 2.0 | 1.6 | 1.6 |
| 11 | | | 4.6 | 1.3 | 1.6 | 1.6 | 1.6 |

An inspection trip in 2004 observed the check dams at Huckleberry Lake to be generally in good condition. Moderate deterioration of mortar capping the check dams was also observed along with moderate rust damage to the valve stem. A few log snags were also present on the saddle check dams. Future maintenance activities will likely consist of rock remortaring, gate valve repair, and removal of log snags.

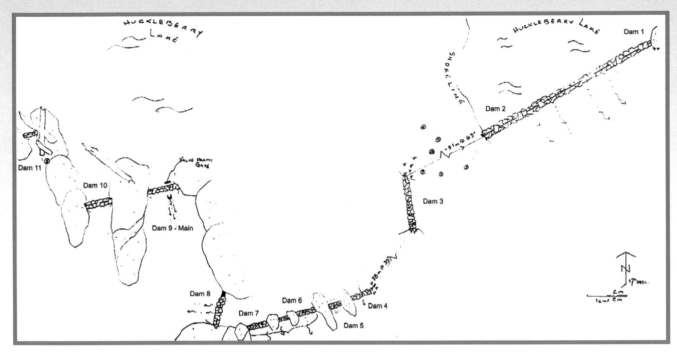

Huckleberry Lake Check Dams Sketch (Modified from and Courtesy of Conners, 1986).

Gate valve at Huckleberry Lake main check dam (10/2005).

One of the 10 saddle check dams at Huckleberry Lake (10/2004). All of the 11 check dams at Huckleberry Lake are very short with the tallest check dam at 3-1/2 feet high.

Huckleberry Lake saddle check dams in 1960 (Courtesy of the USDA Forest Service, Stanislaus National Forest).

Huckleberry Lake main check dam with Fred Tatton and Karl DeFiebre, date unknown; however, possibly in the 1930's (Courtesy of the Tuolumne County Historical Society).

Eastern most saddle check dam at Huckleberry Lake (10/2005).

Huckleberry Lake main check dam (4/1985) before valve replacement (Courtesy of Brian Quelvog).

Repair of a saddle dam at Huckleberry Lake by CDFG (8/1988) with Jim Herrell and Martha Ramsey (Courtesy of Brian Quelvog).

Huckleberry Lake main check dam (8/1988) after CDFG crest repair and mortar replacement project (Courtesy of Brian Quelvog).

# SNOW LAKE

Ten check dams were constructed in 1934 at Snow Lake by the Civilian Conservation Corps. Tom Dahl, a Sonora resident, was one member of the work crew. Due to the relatively flat area of the lake outlet, one main check dam and nine saddle check dams were built between existing granite boulders. The historical literature indicates several different total numbers of saddle check dams which may result from several short saddle dams being considered one dam.

Eight check dams and the gate valve were repaired in 1953-54 by the California Department of Fish and Game (CDFG). An inspection trip by the CDFG in August, 1956 observed that water was spilling over the check dam and that the water flow weir measurement was 6-1/2 inches (Lewis, 1956). A subsequent inspection trip by the CDFG in August, 1958 observed that the lake level was 10 inches below the crest of the check dam and that the dam structure was in good condition (Wilson, 1958).

### Quick Facts

| | |
|---|---|
| Date Constructed: | 1934 |
| Constructed By: | CCC |
| Check Dam Type: | Streamflow |
| Check Dams: | 10 |
| Valve System: | Gate Valve |
| Waterflow Weir: | Yes, 3 foot wide |
| Lake Size: | 40 Acres |
| Drainage: | East Fork of Cherry Creek |
| Elevation: | 9,355 feet |
| Date Repaired: | 1953-54, 1970 |

Snow Lake main dam in summer 2004.

| Dam | Date | Type | Length (ft) | Height (ft) | | Width (ft) | |
|---|---|---|---|---|---|---|---|
| | | | | Upstream | Downstream | Top | Base |
| Total | As Constructed | Main | 46 | 9 | 10 | 2 | 9 |
| 1 | | Saddle | 38.0 | 3.0 | 4.0 | 3.0 | 3.0 |
| 2 | | Main | 15.5 | 5.5 | 7.0 | 3.5 | --- |
| 3 | | | 12.5 | 7.0 | 3.0 | 2.9 | 2.9 |
| 4 | | | 44.0 | 5.0 | 3.4 | 3.5 | 3.5 |
| 5 | 10/11/2004 | | 20.5 | 5.0 | 3.4 | 3.5 | 3.5 |
| 6 | | | 25.0 | 4.3 | 3.5 | 3.5 | 3.5 |
| 7 | | Saddle | 66.5 | 5.0 | --- | 3.5 | 3.5 |
| 8 | | | 16.0 | 0.5 | 2.5 | 2.0 | 2.0 |
| 9 | | | 3.8 | 2.0 | 2.0 | 1.2 | 1.2 |
| 10 | | | 18.6 | 0.8 | 0.9 | 1.2 | 1.2 |

An inspection trip in 2004 observed the check dams at Snow Lake to be in good to poor condition. Significant mortar deterioration on all ten check dams was observed, along with significant leakage within the main check dam. Due to the low water level at that time, additional leakage areas may be present in the check dams. Dam 3, which consists of a mortar filled rock crack, has significant leakage due to mortar degradation. Moderate rust damage was also observed on the gate valve stem. In addition, a water flow measurement weir was in good condition. Future maintenance activities will likely consist of rock remortaring and gate valve repair.

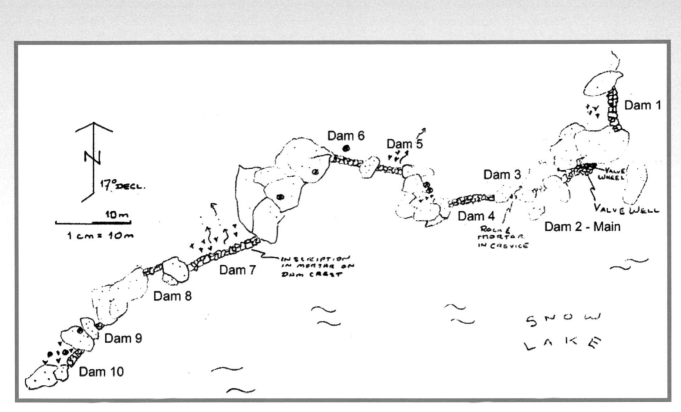

Snow Lake Check Dams Sketch (Modified from and courtesy of Conners, 1986).

Snow Lake check dam site, date unknown – sometime before construction in 1934. Photograph possibly from 1933 inspection trip with Fred Leighton, Dean Hoover, Major Farley, and Ed Burgeson viewing possible check dam sites (Courtesy of the Tuolumne County Historical Society).

Snow Lake check dam during construction (9/1934) with Fred Tatton, Fred Leighton, and Karl DeFiebre (Courtesy of the Tuolumne County Historical Society).

Snow Lake saddle check dam (Dam #7) west of main check dam (8/21/1950), unknown people (Courtesy of the Tuolumne County Historical Society).

Snow Lake construction camp in 1934 during a snow storm (Courtesy of Tom Dahl).

Inscriptions in check dam mortar cap of Dam 7 (10/2004).

Stream flow measurement weir below main check dam (10/2004).

Snow Lake check dam #7 (10/2004).

# COOPER MEADOW

A single check dam at Cooper Meadow was constructed in 1940 by the Civilian Conservation Corps (CCC) as a meadow maintenance dam in an attempt to sub-irrigate the meadow for grazing and meadow enhancement. Quelvog and Conners notes that in 1985, an ungated culvert near the top of the check dam was in poor condition (Conners, 1986). This culvert is not noted in the historical record and was not present in a summer 2004 visit. Frasier indicates the southeast wing of the check dam was built after 1940 (Conners, 1986).

## Quick Facts

| | |
|---|---|
| Date Constructed: | 1940 |
| Constructed By: | CCC |
| Check Dam Type: | Meadow |
| Number of Dams: | 1 |
| Valve System: | None Known |
| Lake Size: | 0 Acres |
| Drainage: | S Fork Stanislaus River |
| Elevation: | 8,360 Feet |

Cooper Meadow check dam in summer 2004.

| Dam | Date | Type | Length (ft) | Height (ft) | | Width (ft) | |
|---|---|---|---|---|---|---|---|
| | | | | Upstream | Downstream | Top | Base |
| Total | As Constructed | --- | ? | ? | ? | ? | ? |
| 1 | 7/3/2004 | Main | 57.5 | 4.5 | 4.5 | 1.5 | 1.5 |

Breached portion of check dam at stream channel (7/2004).

An inspection trip in 2004, observed the check dam at Cooper Meadow in poor condition. A significant portion of the check dam has washed away as shown in the photograph above. A water flow measurement weir and a gate valve or culvert was not present. Future maintenance activities will likely consist of rock replacement, remortaring, and culvert replacement.

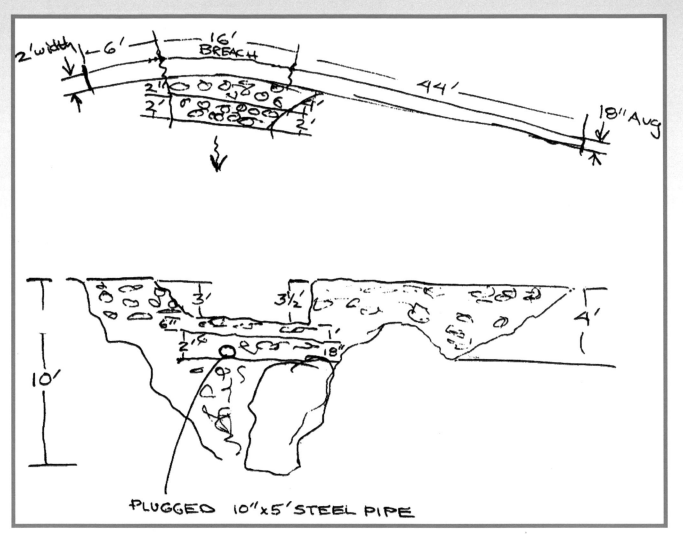

PLUGGED 10"x5' STEEL PIPE

Cooper Meadow Check Dam Sketch (Modified from and courtesy of Conners, 1986).

Cooper Meadow check dam, breached section in stream channel, and stream zone above the check dam (7/2004).

# WHITESIDES MEADOW

Two check dams were constructed at Whitesides Meadow in 1941 by the Civilian Conservation Corps (CCC) in an attempt to sub-irrigate the meadow for grazing and meadow enhancement. The check dams were rebuilt by the Stanislaus National Forest in 1984 and 1985.

**Quick Facts**

| | |
|---|---:|
| Date Constructed: | 1941 |
| Constructed By: | CCC |
| Check Dam Type: | Meadow |
| Number of Dams: | 2 |
| Valve System: | 12 inch pipe |
| Lake Size: | 0 Acres |
| Drainage: | South Fork Stanislaus River |
| Elevation: | 8,780 Feet |
| Date Repaired: | 1984-85 |

Whitesides Meadow main check dam in summer, 2004.

| Dam | Date | Type | Length (ft) | Height (ft) | | Width (ft) | |
|---|---|---|---|---|---|---|---|
| | | | | Upstream | Downstream | Top | Base |
| Total | As Constructed | --- | ? | ? | ? | ? | ? |
| 1 | 7/4/2004 | Main | 92.0 | --- | 9.3 max | 2.5 | 2.5 – 6.0 |
| 2 | | Saddle | 16.8 | 2.2 | 2.2 | 2.8 | 2.8 |

Two tiered main check dam at site of native stream channel (7/2004).

An inspection trip in 2004, observed the Whitesides Meadow check dam in good condition. Slight leakage was present in one saddle check dam as shown above. The spillway area is also in good condition. The repairs made by the Stanislaus National Forest in 1984 and 1985 appear to have held up well. The 12-inch diameter outlet pipe is plugged on the upstream side. Future maintenance activities will likely consist of remortaring, as needed.

Outlet and spillway of main check dam, plugged outlet pipe at left-most base of check dam (7/2004).

Saddle check dam to the south of the main check dam (7/2004).

View of Whitesides Meadow looking east from the check dams (7/2004).

# THE END OF CHECK DAM CONSTRUCTION (1942 – 1951)

While the last check dam would be constructed in the Emigrant Basin at High Emigrant Lake in 1951, support for Leighton's check dams would continue. Many of the prime locations for check dams had already been constructed. Leighton had been able to secure support for the check dams from many organizations and individuals since the beginning, including the Tuolumne County Fish & Game Association, U. S. Forest Service, California Department of Fish and Game, the City and County of San Francisco, Tuolumne County Chamber of Commerce, Tuolumne County Board of Supervisors, local pack stations, the California State Chamber of Commerce, and numerous others who donated labor, money, supplies, and gave support for construction and maintenance of the check dams.

1943 Inspection Trip Party at Camp Yellowhammer (J. R. Hall – Forest Supervisor, Pete Peterson – Stockton Record, R. E. Hartley – Oakdale District, E. R. Huber – U. S. Forest Service, A. C. Taft – California Department of Fish and Game, Byron Curtis – CDFG, Bill Maxwell, Geo Pitts – Photoman, Wm Klenert, Fred Leighton, and Henry Sanguinetti – Packer), 8/29/1943 (Courtesy of the Tuolumne County Historical Society).

An eight-day inspection trip was organized in 1947 by Allen Miller, the Stanislaus National Forest Supervisor and Fred Leighton for the Stream Flow Maintenance Committee of the California State Chamber of Commerce, with representatives from the California Division of Fish & Game, Pacific Gas & Electric Company, California State Automobile Association, Associated Sportsmen of California, U. S. Forest Service, and the Tuolumne County Chamber of Commerce that had originally supported construction of the check dams. The inspection trip started on August 17, 1947 at Leighton Corral above Pinecrest with 24 riders and 12 pack animals, the largest pack group to enter the Stanislaus National Forest at that time (Boss, 1948). It was observed during the inspection trip in the *"driest season in 28 years … an excellent time to observe their* [the check dams] *efficiency"* in that *"in years before these check dams were built, no water was running in"* Cherry Creek and that during this trip the members *"saw countless trout from small fingerlings to 16-inch size"* (Boss, 1948). Leighton Corral is most likely at the site of current Aspen Meadow Pack Station.

The inspection trip members traveled to Cow Meadow where a base camp was established, by way of Crabtree, Bear Lake, Camp Lake, Piute Meadow, and Deer Lake, which provided trips to Y-Meadow Dam, Lertora Lake, Yellowhammer Lake, Lower Buck Lake, and Long Lake (CSCC, 1947). During the fourth day, the inspection party moved to Horse Meadow where a second base camp was established, by way of Emigrant Lake, Emigrant Meadow, Grizzly Peak, Bigelow Lake, and Snow Lake. During the remainder of the trip, the party visited Huckleberry Lake and Wood Lake.

The Stream Flow Maintenance Committee, in their report of the inspection trip, noted that the "*group was quite impressed with the results obtained from the progressive check dam development ... a proven practical method of stream development and water conservation applicable to California conditions has been established ... and ...this Sierra accomplishment is of an effective co-operative effort in meeting the vital need for natural and more practical means in the conservation of water and the propagation of fish and wildlife, erosion, flood control and water conservation*" (CSCC, 1947). The committee also recommended check dam repair, including re-facing or gate replacement at Huckleberry Lake, Y-Meadow Dam, Bear Lake, Lower Buck Lake, Bigelow Lake, and Snow Lake and with the Stanislaus National Forest, recommended construction of check dams at Lunch Meadow, Chain Lake, Grouse Lake, Granite Lake, Piute Ridge, Wire Lake, and Upper Buck Lake.

Leighton was continually looking for new check dam locations and in 1948, developed a report outlining locations for additional check dams. These locations included Upper Buck, Middle Emigrant, Mosquito, Chain, Granite, Grouse, Wire, Shallow, and Piute Ridge Lakes within the Emigrant Basin and Elephant Rock, Summit, and Upper and Lower Highland Lakes in the North Fork of the Stanislaus River drainage. He also suggested constructing a rock-mortar check dam at Leighton Lake to replace the earth-fill dam he had constructed years earlier and to raise existing check dams at Bigelow, Lower Buck, and Bear Lakes (Leighton, 1948).

Leighton and H. O. Pruitt inspected the check dams from August 20th to 25th, 1949 to report on the condition, necessary repairs, and possible location of a new check dam near Mesquite Meadows above Emigrant Lake. They found a 12 acre lake at Mesquite Meadows (probably now known as Mosquito Lake); however, construction of the check dam would be expensive. Due to leakage of water observed on the trip at Bigelow, Emigrant Meadow, Long, and Bear Lakes check dams, Leighton in August 1949 suggested new valve settings to the Stanislaus National Forest (Leighton, 1949), to continue providing the necessary stream flow in late summer. At Bear Lake, Leighton observed that the gate lock was vandalized and that the valve setting should be reduced due to leakage. At Y-Meadow Dam, Leighton observed that the valve stem pipe was disconnected form the gate valve and that the gate valve was partially plugged. At Long Lake, he observed that the valve outlet was entirely plugged and at Lower Buck Lake, the valve outlet was partially plugged and check dam leakage was present. At Cow Meadow and Huckleberry Lakes and Horse Meadow, he observed water was flowing over the top of the check dams. At Snow Lake, he observed that the valve outlet was completely plugged and the valve stem had rusted away and at Bigelow Lake the valve was inadvertently closed. He also observed that check dams at Emigrant Lake and Emigrant Meadow were functioning correctly. (Leighton, 1949).

In 1950, the California Chamber of Commerce passed a resolution praising Leighton's dedication to the check dam project and conservation of natural resources. The resolution stated: "*BE IT RESOLVED that we, the Members of the Central Valley Council, California State Chamber of Commerce, assembled for the Eighty-Fifth Session here in Stockton, this Twenty-Second day of September, 1950, express sincere and deep appreciation to Mr. Fred Leighton of Sonora, Tuolumne County, for his twenty-five years of leadership and valuable service in fostering and expanding the check dam construction program in the Wilderness Area of Tuolumne County. His original idea has spread to many other parts of the State. THEREFORE, the Central Valley Council gratefully acknowledges this proven accomplishment which physically exemplifies a real contribution to the present and future conservation of the Natural Resource of the State of California*" (CSCC, 1950).

Two check dams at Middle Emigrant Lake and High Emigrant Lake would be constructed by the California Department of Fish and Game and the Stanislaus National Forest in 1951. These would be the last check dams to be constructed in the Emigrant Basin due to dwindling support and that many lakes already had existing check dams.

# MIDDLE EMIGRANT LAKE

Three check dams were constructed at Middle Emigrant Lake in 1951 by the California Department of Fish and Game (CDFG) and the Stanislaus National Forest as a streamflow maintenance dam.

An inspection trip by the CDFG in August, 1956 observed water flowing over the check dam (Lewis, 1956). A subsequent inspection trip by the CDFG in August, 1958 observed water flowing over the check dam with a few snow banks on the east side of the lake (Wilson, 1958).

## Quick Facts

| | | | |
|---|---|---|---|
| Date Constructed: | 1951 | Waterflow Weir: | Yes |
| Constructed By: | USFS & CDFG | Lake Size: | 18 Acres |
| Check Dam Type: | Streamflow | Drainage: | North Fork of Cherry Creek |
| Number of Dams: | 3 | Elevation: | 9,335 Feet |
| Valve System: | Gate Valve/Pipe (outlet obscured) | Date Repaired: | Unknown |

| Dam | Date | Type | Length (ft) | Height (ft) | | Width (ft) | |
|---|---|---|---|---|---|---|---|
| | | | | Upstream | Downstream | Top | Base |
| Total | As Constructed | --- | 36 | 5 | 6-1/2 | 1-1/2 | 6 |
| 1 | | Main | 46.7 | 0.9 – 6.3 | 1.0 – 6.3 | 1.6 – 3.9 | --- |
| 2 | 10/16/2004 | Saddle | 12.0 | 1.0 | 1.2 | 1.2 | 1.2 |
| 3 | | | 9.6 | 0.8 | 0.6 | 1.8 | 1.8 |

An inspection trip in 2004, observed the Middle Emigrant Lake check dam in poor condition. A breached area exists to the east of the valve well as shown in the photograph above. The gate valve stem is in very poor condition due to rusting and the outlet pipe is obscured by rock debris. A broken water flow measurement weir is present below the check dam. Future maintenance activities should consist of rock replacement, remortaring, and gate valve replacement.

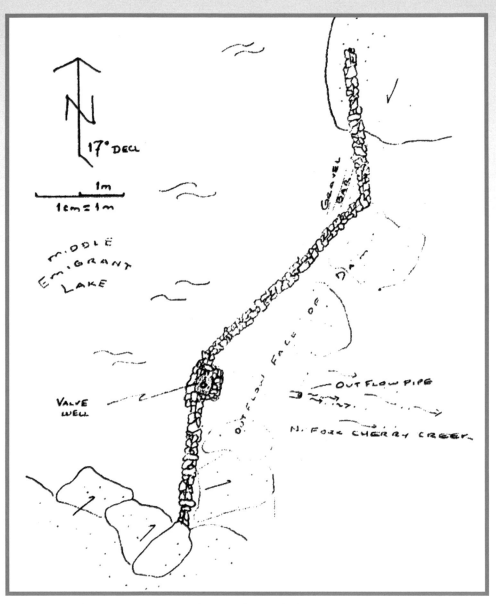

Middle Emigrant Main Check Dam Sketch (Modified from and courtesy of Conners, 1986).

Middle Emigrant Lake check dam valve well, partially breached portion of main dam to upper right of valve well (10/2004).

Middle Emigrant valve well and gate valve (4/1985) with extensive sedimentation within valve well (Courtesy of Brian Quelvog).

Middle Emigrant Lake water flow measurement weir (8/1984) with wooden boards in place (Courtesy of Brian Quelvog). Weir has since deteriorated.

Middle Emigrant Lake main check dam to east of valve well (7/1987) before partial breach (Courtesy of Brian Quelvog).

Stream flow measurement weir downstream from main dam (10/2004).

Middle Emigrant Lake and check dam (10/2004).

Breached portion of main check dam (Courtesy of Ernie Marino).

# HIGH EMIGRANT LAKE

The High Emigrant Lake check dam was constructed in 1951 by the Stanislaus National Forest and the California Department of Fish and Game (CDFG) as a streamflow maintenance dam on the North Fork of Cherry Creek.

An inspection trip by the CDFG in August, 1956 observed that water was flowing over the top of the check dam, that the mine road had washed out, and that earlier repair work appeared satisfactory (Lewis, 1956). Leighton, while on this trip, recommended changing the release to 90 days from 100 days. During a subsequent inspection trip by the CDFG in August, 1958, the lake level was even with the top of the check dam, a weir was present, and the dam structure was in good condition (Wilson, 1958). Major repairs were made on the check dam in 1955 and an instruction tag was placed on the valve in 1970 by the CDFG (Quelvog, 1986). Quelvog noted that a weir was present as early as 1958; however, inspection in 2004 and earlier years failed to discover the location of the flow weir. Recent vandalism has rendered the gate valve inoperable, resulting in the protective valve well to fill with sediment.

### Quick Facts

| | |
|---|---:|
| Date Constructed: | 1951 |
| Constructed By: | USFS & CDFG |
| Check Dam Type: | Meadow |
| Number of Dams: | 1 |
| Valve System: | Gate Valve/8" Pipe |
| Lake Size: | 10 Acres |
| Drainage: | North Fork Cherry Creek |
| Elevation: | 9,706 Feet |
| Date Repaired: | 1955, 1970, 1973-74 |

High Emigrant Lake check dam in summer 2004.

| Dam | Date | Type | Length (ft) | Height (ft) | | Width (ft) | |
|---|---|---|---|---|---|---|---|
| | | | | Upstream | Downstream | Top | Base |
| Total | As Constructed | --- | 46 | 8-1/2 | 11-1/2 | 1-1/2 | 9-1/2 |
| 1 | 10/10/2004 | Main | 61.5 | --- | 7.0 | 6.0 | 10.0 |

An inspection trip in 2004 observed the High Emigrant Lake check dam in poor condition. The gate valve has been vandalized and the valve well has filled with sediment. Several mortared rocks in the spillway area have been removed with a pry bar, as evidenced by tool marks in the remaining mortar. Rocks are also missing from the valve well. Extensive leakage through the dam was also observed. No water flow measurement weir was present. Future maintenance activities should consist of rock replacement, remortaring, and complete gate valve replacement.

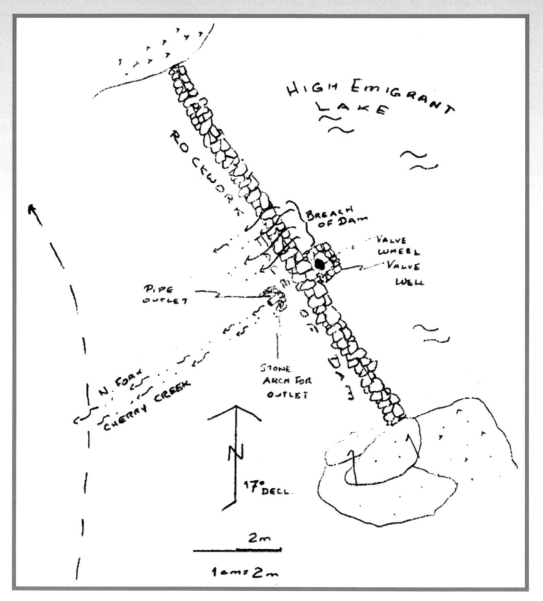

High Emigrant Lake Check Dam Sketch (Modified from and courtesy of Conners, 1986).

High Emigrant Lake check dam in summer 1954 by George Burnett, USFS Regional Office, during a recreational management inspection trip (Courtesy of the USDA Forest Service, Stanislaus National Forest). Note spillway at left of protective valve well and generally good condition of the check dam.

High Emigrant Lake in August, 1984. Check dam is in generally good condition with moderate leakage present (Courtesy of Brian Quelvog).

High Emigrant Lake check dam in 1960. Note spillway at right of protective valve well and generally good condition of the check dam (Courtesy of the USDA Forest Service, Stanislaus National Forest).

Vandalized gate valve and protective valve well (10/2004). Due to inoperable gate valve, coarse disintegrated granite (DG) sediment has filled the remains of the valve well.

High Emigrant Lake check dam (6/1998) under an impending summer storm. Check dam and spillway in generally good condition. One area of leakage is present to the left of the outlet area.

High Emigrant Lake check dam (6/1998) with intact gate valve and valve well. Old mining access road from Leavitt Lake to Snow Lake in background, now used as a trail.

High Emigrant Lake check dam with spillway at left center (10/2004). No evidence of a waterflow weir was present in the stream below.

# CHECK DAM MAINTENANCE ACTIVITIES (1952 – 1975)

The California Department of Fish & Game (CDFG) started involvement with Leighton's check dams in the early 1930's; however, it was not until the early 1950's that they become intimately involved with the check dams. Starting as early as 1954, the CDFG actively conducted routine site visits to the check dams, coordinated with California Division of Safety of Dams for permit inspections of the check dams, and made numerous repairs to the check dams.

A meeting was held at the Stanislaus National Forest headquarters in Sonora on March 21, 1952 with the Stanislaus National Forest, Fred Leighton, and C. K. Fisher and Terrance Potter of the California Department of Fish and Game to discuss plans for stream flow maintenance dams, as the check dams came to be known. During this meeting, it was decided that the highest priority projects were at: Bigelow, Lower Buck, Bear, Emigrant, and Leighton Lakes and Lower Highland, Wheeler, and Grouse Lakes outside the Emigrant Basin (Potter, 1952). It was decided that the check dam at Bigelow Lake would be raised 3 feet and that an overflow check dam at Bigelow Lake not be constructed due to insufficient water storage, that raising the Lower Buck Lake check dam was a very good project, and that the Bear Lake check dam should be raised 2 feet. In addition, they recommended that the Emigrant Lake check dam should be raised 1 foot, that the Leighton Lake check dam be raised 4 feet, that proposed check dams at Wire Lake and Chain Lakes be further studied, and proposed check dams at Mesquite (probably Mosquito Lake today) and Upper and Lower Lunch Meadow be abandoned (Potter, 1952).

One of the many inspection trips to observe the check dams was organized by the California Department of Fish & Game in 1956. On August 20, 1956, a group including Seth Gordon, Bob Calkins, Bob Paul, Leo Shapovalov, Bob Lewis, Andy Weaver, and George Magladry of the CDFG; Fred Leighton; Jess Hall; A. Starker Leopold of the Sierra Club; Edward Sipe of the State Chamber of Commerce; Fred Cronmiller, Russell McRory, and Allen McCready of the U. S. Forest Service; Vernon Rue, a local sportsman; and packer Doug Wittde left Pinecrest for Camp Yellowhammer (Lewis, 1956). On the trip to Camp Yellowhammer the first day, the group traveled past Bear, Y-Meadow, Long, Lower Buck, and Leighton Lakes. One the second day, the group traveled to Yellowhammer and Big Lakes, observing one of the original check dams at Yellowhammer Lake and on the third day traveled to Cow Meadow, Huckleberry, Bigelow, Snow, High Emigrant, Emigrant Meadow, and Middle Emigrant Lakes. On August 24, 1956, the group returned to Pinecrest, by way of Emigrant Lake.

During the trip, gate valves were flushed and the flow adjusted to conditions needed, along with documenting any repair that was needed on the check dams. Leighton suggested that the Bear Lake check dam be raised 12 inches so water would flow over a rock area near the check dam to prevent water flow and logs from going over the dam. Logs and debris going over the check dam was causing severe damage to the check dam. The party observed that only 25 to 30% of the main check dam at Cow Meadow Lake was remaining, even through the dam was built with reinforcing metal rebar and some erosion had occurred at the Leighton Lake check dam from high water flows (Lewis, 1956).

At a meeting after the trip, it was recorded that A. Starker Leopold, son of Aldo Leopold, an early conservationist, "*was quite impressed by the work being done on flow maintenance dams and also by the sub-irrigation of meadows brought about by permanent level dams such as Cow Meadow, Horse Meadow, Yellowhammer and Huckleberry*" and while speaking for himself and not the Sierra Club who he represented, was "*going to make an effort to explain more fully the work being done with flow maintenance dams and permanent level dams to members and directors of the Sierra Club*" (Lewis, 1956).

In addition, the trip members agreed that the Cow Meadow check dam would be rebuilt and two small repair jobs would be performed at Huckleberry Lake in 1957 (Lewis, 1956). The CDFG direction would "*then be to maintain this area with necessary repair and divert additional work into other areas in the Sierras that are in need of stream flow maintenance dams*" (Lewis, 1956).

On an annual inspection trip in 1958, Malcolm E. Wilson, a CDFG fisheries manager, and two seasonal aids inspected nine of the check dams. During the August trip, the group noted that check dams at Middle Emigrant, High Emigrant, Snow, Emigrant, Lower Buck, and Long Lakes were all in good condition and check dams at Emigrant Meadow and Bigelow Lakes and at Horse Meadow were all in fair condition (Lewis, 1958).

The table below details the site visits, California Department of Water Resources – Division of Dam Safety permit inspections, and repair or maintenance performed on the Emigrant Basin check dams by the California Department of Fish & Game from 1954 to 1975. As the check dams aged and dam safety became more of a concern in California, the Division of Safety of Dams (DSOD) became more involved in check dam inspection activities.

| Check Dam | Year of CDFG Related Check Dam Inspections and Repairs | | | | | | | |
|---|---|---|---|---|---|---|---|---|
| | 1954-57 | 1956 | 1958 | 1964 | 1970 | 1972 | 1973-74 | 1975 |
| Bear Lake | V | V | --- | --- | --- | --- | --- | --- |
| Bigelow Lake | V | V | V | --- | R | I | --- | V |
| Cooper Meadow | --- | --- | --- | --- | --- | --- | --- | --- |
| Cow Meadow Lake | --- | V | --- | --- | --- | --- | --- | --- |
| Emigrant Lake | V | V | V | V | R | --- | --- | V |
| Emigrant Meadow Lake | --- | V | V | V | R | --- | --- | V |
| High Emigrant Lake | --- | V | V | V | R | I | R | V |
| Horse Meadow | --- | --- | V | V | --- | --- | --- | --- |
| Huckleberry Lake | --- | V | --- | --- | --- | --- | --- | V |
| Leighton Lake | --- | V | --- | --- | --- | --- | --- | --- |
| Long Lake | --- | V | V | V | R | --- | --- | --- |
| Lower Buck Lake | V | V | V | V | R | I | R | V |
| Middle Emigrant Lake | --- | V | V | V | --- | --- | --- | V |
| Red Can Lake | --- | --- | --- | --- | --- | --- | --- | --- |
| Snow Lake | --- | V | V | V | R | --- | --- | --- |
| Whitesides Meadow | --- | --- | --- | --- | --- | --- | --- | --- |
| Yellowhammer Lake | --- | --- | --- | --- | --- | --- | --- | --- |
| Y-Meadow Dam | --- | V | --- | V | --- | --- | --- | --- |

Type of Check Dam Inspection and Maintenance V – CDFG Site Visit, I – DSOD Inspection, and R – Repair (Quelvog, 2005; others).

The check dams have been operated by a variety of groups, beginning with Fred Leighton, then the U. S. Forest Service, and then the California Department of Fish and Game (CDFG). This dual operation of check dams was questioned in 1971 by the CDFG who operated the check dams in the Emigrant Basin under a special use permit from the U. S. Forest Service. The CDFG operated all the check dams with the exception of Y-Meadow, Bear, Huckleberry, and Leighton Lakes (CDFG, 1971). The CDFG was willing to operate and maintain all of the Emigrant Basin check dams if the U. S. Forest Service would repair the dams it maintained to a good condition.

The first known inspections of the check dams made by the Division of Safety of Dams (DSOD) occurred in 1972 at Bigelow (#1-26), Lower Buck (#1-25), and High Emigrant Lakes (#1-27), the only check dams to fall under DSOD jurisdiction. While the DSOD found the check dams to be safe for continued use, they did indicate that due to deterioration of mortar in the check dams, maintenance was advised and leakage through the check dams was present at Bigelow and High Emigrant Lakes (DSOD, 1971). The DSOD regulates all non-federal dams in California with a storage capacity greater than 50 acre-feet and/or height greater than 25 feet.

Gate valves at Lower Buck and High Emigrant Lakes were opened fully by Larry Dunn on August 29, 1973, and the Lower Buck Lake check dam was repaired by the California Department of Fish and Game by replacing rocks and mortar in September, 1974 at a cost of $1,078 (Dunn, 1973; Mills, 1974). A check dam at High Emigrant Lake was also repaired by the CDFG in 1974.

An inspection trip in 1975 by the California Division of Fish and Game found leakage occurring at High Emigrant Lake in the same places before the 1974 repair, the check dams at Emigrant Meadow and Emigrant Lakes were in excellent condition; however, they were missing valve stems, the check dam at Middle Emigrant Lake was in good condition, and the repairs to the check dam at Lower Buck Lake had held up well (Mills, 1975).

# THE FORMATION OF THE EMIGRANT WILDERNESS (1964 – 1975)

The beginning of forming a designated wilderness in the Emigrant Basin area emanated from the original establishment of the Emigrant Basin Primitive Area on April 23, 1931 by the U. S. Forest Service (NPS, 1938) under Regulation L-20. An area of 98,043 acres, including 1,055 acres of non-Federal land was included in the designated Emigrant Basin Primitive Area (Senate, 1974).

The federal Wilderness Act of 1964 defined wilderness as "*an area of undeveloped Federal land retaining its primeval character and influence, without permanent improvements or human habitation, which is protected and managed so as to preserve its natural conditions and which (1) generally appears to have been affected primarily by the forces of nature, with the imprint of man's work substantially unnoticeable; (2) has outstanding opportunities for solitude or a primitive and unconfined type of recreation; (3) has at least five thousand acres of land or is sufficient size as to make practicable its preservation and use in an unimpaired condition' and (4) may also contain ecological, geological, or other features of scientific, educational, scenic, or historical value*" and that "*wilderness area shall be devoted to the public purposes of recreational, scenic, scientific, educational, conservation, and historical use*" (16 USC 1131-1136). This congressional legislation would lead federal land management agencies to investigate and classify administered lands that might qualify as wilderness. It should be noted that the original act and legislation that followed included the ideas of recreational, conservation, and historical use.

The original proposal for establishment of the Emigrant Wilderness was published on July 18, 1969 by the U. S. Forest Service (USFS, 1969) detailed areas to be included within the proposed wilderness area, including a "*90,566 acre portion of the existing Emigrant Basin Primitive Area, 15,388 acres of adjoining [USFS] land, and 1,034 acres of private land*" to be acquired and two excluded areas: one 380 acre area adjacent to Relief Reservoir and the second, a 6,443 acre area containing tungsten mines and claims near Snow Lake and Horse Meadow. This proposal would create a contiguous 106,988 acre Emigrant Wilderness. The proposal only makes a brief reference to the check dams and stated that "*other developments, not conforming to Wilderness in these parcels, includes various cabins, several flow maintenance dams, and concrete weirs*" were present (USFS, 1969). At this time, the definition of wilderness was still being arduously debated by federal land management agencies.

Memorial sign to Fred Leighton in 1964 at Camp Yellowhammer. Sign was removed by the U. S. Forest Service due to wilderness conflict concerns and now resides on the front of the Strawberry Store in Strawberry, California (Courtesy of the USDA Forest Service, Stanislaus National Forest),

The U. S. Forest Service Emigrant Wilderness proposal and President Richard Nixon's subsequent Emigrant Wilderness proposal to Congress led Representative Harold (Biz) Johnson whose California district included the area of the proposed wilderness area, to introduce a bill designating the Emigrant Wilderness (H.R. 3142, 93rd Congress) on January 29, 1973. This bill referred directly to the USFS Emigrant Wilderness Proposal drafted earlier; however, his bill only included the 105,876 acres of USFS administered land. This bill was subsequently added to bill H.R. 5422 (93rd Congress), incorporating numerous other wilderness establishment proposals nationwide. At the same time, Senator Henry M. Jackson introduced a bill (S. 601, 93rd Congress) essentially similar to bill H.R. 3142, except for a change in acreage to a proposed 106,899 acre Emigrant Wilderness. Senator Jackson's S. 601 bill was the same as the President's earlier Emigrant Wilderness submittal to Congress. California Senators Alan Cranston and John V. Tunney also introduced a separate bill (S. 111, 93rd Congress) in the Senate proposing an 113,000 acre wilderness area (Senate, 1974). Bill H.R. 5422 was incorporated into bill H.R. 12884 (93rd Congress) with additional wilderness designation proposals on February 19, 1974 that eventually created the Emigrant Wilderness with the passage of Public Law 93-632 (93rd Congress) on January 3, 1975.

During the time leading up to the enabling Emigrant Wilderness legislation, hearings by the House of Representatives Subcommittee on Public Lands of the Committee on Interior and Insular Affairs were conducted to "*find out about both sides*" of the issue of establishing new wilderness areas (HR, 1973). Speakers at these hearings included Representatives Harold Johnson and Jerome Waldie, Senator Alan Cranston, Department of Agriculture Deputy Chief for Administration (Forest Service) Jack W. Deinema, Wilderness Society representative Harry Crandell, and UC Berkeley geology professor Dr. Clyde Wahrhaftig. Statements made by these speakers shed light on the early legislative position related to the check dams. During these hearings it was clear that the members did not consider the check dams to be a significant intrusion of wilderness; however, marked disagreement existed about the proposed exclusion area near Snow Lake and the Sierran crest for tungsten mining activity.

Representative Johnson, who introduced the original Emigrant Wilderness establishment bill, stated during his testimony that:

"*through continual careful management and selective use of resources, its ruggedness and beauty as well as its primitive quality [has] been preserved*", that the area "*is an important watershed ... and ... one can easily experience the challenges and solitude of wilderness*" and that "*small masonry and concrete dams have been constructed inconspicuously to increase water storage and facilitate uniform flows in lower streams*" (HR, 1973).

Senator Alan Cranston reiterated the minor visual impact of the check dams in his statement during the hearings "*I am also aware that there are some small inconspicuous flow maintenance dams made of natural rock and covered with moss and lichens in the excluded area. These are substantially unnoticeable and do not detract from the wilderness quality of the area*" and that none "*of these minor non-conforming features should preclude wilderness designation of the entire 113,000 acres as the Emigrant Wilderness*" (HR, 1973). Additionally, Senator Cranston stated "*... within this area are ... some inconspicuous flow maintenance dams made of natural rock and covered with moss and lichens. These are substantially unnoticeable and like the snow cabins and snow courses in the area proposed by the Forest Service do not detract from the wilderness quality of Emigrant Basin*" (Senate, 1974).

Even Jack Deinema, the Forest Service officer representing the official position of the department during the hearings, conferred with the low impact of the check dams, stating "*there are several existing uses in the area that keep it from being completely untrammeled, or there are noticeable improvements. There are weirs, for example, and there are seven snow courses; there are some flow-check dams put out by the State fish and game department within the area*". When asked by the committee if the improvements would be consistent with the objective of the Wilderness Act, Mr. Deinema agreed and added that the Forest Service "*feel[s] that they can be provided for within the administrative provisions*" (HR, 1973).

While the Wilderness Society did not specifically mention the check dams during testimony, they did not indicate any objection to the existing structures, except those associated with existing mining activity near Snow Lake and stated "*the imprint of man's work is barely discernable, and, in a few spots where it exists, is impermanent*" (HR, 1973).

In his testimony mainly related to the area geology, Dr. Wahrhaftig did not comment specifically on the check dams; however, he did note that he did not know of any "... *water-storage capability that would justify excluding any of this area*" and the "*Forest Service cabin in Horse Meadow and the Snow Survey Cabin at Summit Meadow are, in my opinion, perfectly conforming structures in the wilderness*" (HR, 1973).

A House of Representatives report on bill H.R. 12884 stated that "*water production is important and this will not be curtailed. Certain small weirs and flow dams are present, but are essentially unnoticeable ... the weirs and small dams will likewise by retained*" (HR, 1974). A Senate committee report on a similar bill stated that:

> "*Within this area of 100,000 acres are several manmade developments. There are two well-hidden snow cabins, seven well-distributed snow-measuring courses, and several cabins and barns for managing livestock. Except for the inconspicuous snow cabins and snow courses, the other structures will be removed within 10 years after the area is classified as Wilderness. In addition, there are a number of small, inconspicuous flow-maintenance dams and weirs made of natural rock and covered with moss and lichens. They are substantially unnoticeable*" (Senate, 1974). It was the opinion of the Committee on Interior and Insular Affairs that "*we feel that each of the areas [bill entailed numerous wilderness area proposals] proposed for wilderness designation meets the definition of wilderness as contained in subsection 2(c) of the Wilderness Act*" (Senate, 1974).

During development of bill S. 600 (93rd Congress) related to designating National Wildlife Refuge lands as wilderness, the Committee on Interior and Insular Affairs did not intend that all structures existing within proposed wilderness areas be removed upon wilderness designation:

> "*in a few situations where improvements now exist, the Committee was assured by the Department witnesses that these were scheduled for removal upon wilderness designation. This removal commitment does not, of course, apply to those structures or improvements which have historical, scientific, or safety values. Also in a few locations, certain long established and existing uses, such as controlled burning, were recognized by the Committee as necessary and acceptable,*

> *under carefully controlled conditions, for the use, safety, and enjoyment of these areas*" (Senate, 1974).

The Emigrant Wilderness was designated on January 3, 1975 (USFS, 2003) by Congress and President Nixon in Public Law 93-632, incorporating the 98,043 acre Emigrant Basin Primitive Area and other areas adjacent to the existing primitive area, but excluding the area near Snow Lake. In relation to the Emigrant Wilderness, the legislation stated:

> "*Sec 2. In accordance with subsection 3(b) of the Wilderness Act (8 Stat. 891; 16 U.S.C. 1132) the following areas are hereby designated as wilderness and, therefore, as components of the National Wilderness Preservation System:*

> *(b) The area in the Stanislaus National Forest in California classified as the Emigrant Basin Primitive Area, with additions thereto and deletions there from, which area comprises approximately one hundred and six thousand nine hundred and ten acres, is generally depicted on a map entitled "Emigrant Wilderness – Proposed, 1970" on file in the office of the Chief, Forest Service, Department of Agriculture, and shall be known as the Emigrant Wilderness. The area commonly called the Cherry Creek exclusion, depicted on such map as Exclusion 2 and comprising approximately six thousand and forty-two acres, shall, in accordance with the provisions of subsection 3(d) of the Wilderness Act, be reviewed by the Secretary of Agriculture as to its suitability or nonsuitability for preservation as wilderness in conjunction with his review of the potential addition to the Hoover Wilderness in the Toiyabe National Forest. The recommendations of the President to the Congress on the potential addition to the Hoover Wilderness shall be accompanied by the President's recommendations on the Cherry Creek Exclusion. The previous classification of the Emigrant Basin Primitive Area is hereby abolished with the exception of said Exclusion 2*".

The establishment of the Emigrant Wilderness area would forever change the management of the Emigrant Basin area and prevent new check dams from being built. The establishment also started extensive disagreements about the disposition of the check dams between the U. S. Forest Service, sportsmen, and environmental organizations that continue to this day.

# THE CONTROVERSY OVER LEIGHTON'S CHECK DAM LEGACY (1975 – PRESENT)

Fred Leighton's enduring legacy of conservation in the high Sierra with the use of check dams continues to this day. With the establishment of the Emigrant Wilderness in 1975, including the lack of unquestionable direction as to the disposition of the check dams in legislation, controversy surrounds the 18 check dams due to the perceived compatibility issues with wilderness legislation and often differing ideology and definition of "wilderness".

One concept that appears to have been overlooked in the current controversy is the real impact of man on Earth and an overriding perspective if a true wilderness can exist. In Mann and Plummer's recent book (1996), they stated: "*Because [Native Americans] were a major ecological factor in North America, their removal did not create a wilderness, in the sense of place untrammeled by the presence of humanity. Wilderness has not existed in North America for at least ten thousand years; the idea that people are not a part of the ecological picture … 'is itself a human artifact' – a cultural myth*".

Subsequent to the establishment of the Emigrant Wilderness in 1975, an Emigrant Wilderness Management Plan, required by the enabling legislation, was prepared in 1979. The management plan included such comments related to the check dams as "*these dams blend with the landscape*", "*there are three meadow dams built to slow erosion and maintain good forage*", and that "*these dams were described in the wilderness proposal sent to Congress and were not directed to be removed in the subsequent classification action*" (USFS, 1979).

The 1979 management plan also required a study to determine "*the condition, value and cost-effectiveness of the various check dams as well as their effects on the natural hydrological processes*" (USFS, 1979). This study culminated in 1989, as an Environmental Assessment (EA), after 5 years of work and was based on a concurrent study: *Water Control Structures in the Emigrant Wilderness – Study Report*. The EA considered four alternatives in detail, including: Alternative 1) No Action, Alternative 2) Retain all Existing Water Control Structures, Alternative 3) Retain High Value Structures and Phase Out Others, and Alternative 4) Phase Out All Water Control Structures (USFS, 1989). Alternative 3 would have retained check dams at Bigelow Lake, Cow Meadow Lake, Emigrant Lake, Emigrant Meadow Lake, Huckleberry Lake, Leighton Lake, Horse Meadow, Snow Lake, and Whitesides Meadow. As part of the public comments invited as part of the EA process, the Tuolumne County Historical Society supported retaining "*all dams (repair and reconstruct as needed)*" (TCHS, 1989). The Tuolumne Group of the Sierra Club initially supported retaining and maintaining some dams due to their "*historical significance … and they were not now a significant intrusion of man on the wilderness*", but then reversed their position to favor "*gradual deterioration of all the dams without maintenance*" (TGSC, undated).

On September 28, 1984, an additional 6,100 acres was added to the Emigrant Wilderness by the California Wilderness Act of 1984, including the previously excluded area near Snow Lake, resulting in the current size of the wilderness area. The Act also restated the administration provision of the original Wilderness Act of 1964, in that "*as provided in section 4(b) of the Wilderness Act, the Secretary concerned shall administer such areas so as to preserve their wilderness character and to devote them to the public purposes of recreational, scenic, scientific, educational, conservation, and historical use*" (PL 98-425).

In November 1989, the Stanislaus National Forest Supervisor signed a Decision Notice and Finding of No Significant Impact statement that selected Alternative 3 as "*the dam study determined that some structures have resource values which make them desirable to retain at this time while others do not … recognizes the NRHP properties as a theme of water conservation practices of a past era … dams at lakes with high recreation and angling use are retained as a desirable combination of values … provide a small, more manageable system of dams … the three meadow dams … have an insignificant improvement on sub-irrigation and fish habitat ,,, and nearly all the opinion favoring the dams centered on historic and fishery values*" (USFS, 1989). Surprisingly, Joyce Muroaka, the USFS Regional Forester revered the Forest Supervisor's Decision Notice on April 29, 1990 and required the check dams to be removed within five years, only to change her decision two days later due to the outpouring of support of local citizens and moved the final decision and ultimate fate of the check dams back locally to the Stanislaus National Forest.

Leighton's Yellowhammer Camp and three check dams at Leighton, Emigrant, and Lower Buck Lakes were nominated for inclusion in the National

Register of Historic Places (NRHP) in August 1980 and subsequently resubmitted in June 1982 by the Stanislaus National Forest. The California State Historic Preservation Office (SHPO) approved the nomination; however, the nomination papers were lost in Washington, D.C, pending federal approval. Due to other commitments on the Stanislaus National Forest, the nomination process was not continued (Supernowicz, 1988).

Yellowhammer Camp consists of an older cabin built in 1922 on the site of an earlier cabin built in the 1890's, a newer cabin built in 1958, a cookhouse built prior to 1951, a barn and corral, and four outbuildings (Conners, 1986) and was used by Leighton each summer during check dam construction, inspection, and maintenance trips.

In 1988, a second study to determine if any of the check dams were eligible for NRHP listing was completed and determined that check dams at Bigelow, Emigrant Meadow, and Long Lakes, along with the previously nominated check dams at Leighton, Lower Buck, and Emigrant Lakes were eligible for listing in the NRHP as having contributed to events in local history, were associated with significant individuals of the past, and retain their original integrity. The study noted that "*the efforts of Leighton and others to modify streamflows for fishery improvement may not meet today's standards of wilderness use, yet many of the idea of streamflow maintenance dams and their subsequent development resulted in a significant contribution to the development of outdoor recreation and fisheries habitat improvement within California*" (Supernowicz, 1988). The California SHPO office concurred with this second determination for eligibility of check dams at Bigelow, Long, Emigrant Meadow, Emigrant, Leighton, and Lower Buck Lakes for inclusion in the NRHP on November 14, 1988 (Gualteri, 1988). However, the check dams are still not listed in the NRHP, even though they are eligible.

The California Department of Fish & Game initially responded to the study by actively supporting the check dams and stated "*their importance to the fishery is well documents and we believe their role in management cannot be duplicated via aerial plants*" and "*we propose including all of the existing structures under our use permit in order to maintain a solid, consistent program for fish and wildlife in the coming decades*" (Nokes, 1989). Once the study report was available, the CDFG continued support for the check dams, "*even though they are non-*

*conforming structures they were present prior to wilderness designation and can remain under wilderness designation*" (Nokes, 1989). They assumed that Alternative 3 would be selected by the U. S. Forest Service that phased out some check dams, including those at Snow and High Emigrant Lakes; however, they requested that both of the check dams be maintained.

The next phase of determining the fate of the check dams came in October 1991, when the Stanislaus National Forest issued a new Land and Resources Management Plan. This management plan called for development of a new Emigrant Wilderness Management Plan that culminated into the Emigrant Wilderness Management Direction Environmental Impact Statement (EIS). A Record of Decision for the EIS was signed in April 1998 by the Forest Supervisor (USFS, 1998). Due to 14 appeals of the decision, the USFS Regional Forester issued an appeal review decision and the Stanislaus National Forest revised the management plan into the current Emigrant Wilderness Management Direction (USFS, 2002). The current Emigrant Wilderness Management Plan directed that "*maintenance of water impoundment structures [check dams] will be consistent with the Forest Service/CDFG joint strategy*" ... *dams without a high enough value to warrant retention should be allowed to deteriorate naturally (no maintenance) consistent with FSM [Forest Service Manual] direction, rather than removed ... if a safety concern dictates removal, conduct the appropriate level of analysis to determine removal method*" (USFS, 2002).

The Forest Service/CDFG joint strategy was developed in November 2000 by the USFS Regional Forester and the California Division of Fish and Game (CDFG) Director "*to work toward collaborative solutions to meet the needs and concerns of both agencies*" (Powell, 2000) in terms of the check dams. This Joint Strategy recommended to maintain check dams at Long, Lower Buck, Leighton, Emigrant Meadow, Middle Emigrant, Emigrant, Bigelow, and Huckleberry Lakes, not to maintain the remainder of the check dams, that "*both agencies favor naturally reproducing fisheries to reduce impacts on natural processes*", and to "*further evaluate potential impacts to aquatic and riparian species*" (Powell, 2000). As to potential vandalism, the joint strategy committed that the "*USFS will work cooperatively with interested parties to either rebuild portions of dams, which are destroyed due to vandalism, or remove unauthorized repairs on dams*" (Powell, 2005).

While disagreements continued as to the fate of the check dams, the California Department of Fish & Game (CDFG) kept near yearly site visits of the check dams, coordinated with the Division of Safety of Dams (DSOD) on permit inspections, and some repair work from 1979 to 1996.

| Check Dam | Year of CDFG Related Check Dam Inspections and Repair | | | | | | | | | | | | | |
|---|---|---|---|---|---|---|---|---|---|---|---|---|---|---|
| | 76 | 77 | 80 | 81 | 84 | 85 | 86 | 88 | 89 | 90 | 91 | 92 | 93 | 96 |
| Bear Lake | --- | --- | --- | --- | V | V | --- | --- | --- | V | --- | --- | --- | --- |
| Bigelow Lake | --- | I | V | I | I | V | --- | V | V | V | I | --- | I | I |
| Cooper Meadow | --- | --- | V | --- | V | V | --- | V | V | V | --- | --- | --- | --- |
| Cow Meadow Lake | --- | --- | V | --- | V | V | --- | V | V | V | --- | --- | --- | --- |
| Emigrant Lake | --- | --- | V | --- | V | V | V | --- | V | V | I | V | I | I |
| Emigrant Meadow Lake | --- | --- | V | --- | V | V | --- | V | V | V | --- | V | --- | --- |
| High Emigrant Lake | --- | I | V | I | I | V | --- | V | V | V | I | V | I | I |
| Horse Meadow | --- | --- | V | --- | V | V | --- | V | V | V | --- | --- | --- | --- |
| Huckleberry Lake | --- | --- | V | --- | V | V | --- | R | V | V | --- | --- | --- | --- |
| Leighton Lake | R | --- | V | --- | V | V | --- | V | V | V | --- | --- | --- | --- |
| Long Lake | --- | --- | V | --- | V | V | V | V | V | V | --- | --- | --- | --- |
| Lower Buck Lake | --- | I | V | R | I | V | --- | R | V | V | I | --- | I | I |
| Middle Emigrant Lake | --- | --- | V | --- | V | V | --- | V | V | V | I | V | --- | --- |
| Red Can Lake | --- | --- | --- | --- | V | V | --- | V | V | V | --- | --- | --- | --- |
| Snow Lake | --- | --- | --- | --- | V | V | --- | V | V | V | I | --- | --- | --- |
| Whitesides Meadow | --- | --- | --- | --- | V | V | --- | V | V | V | --- | --- | --- | --- |
| Yellowhammer Lake | --- | --- | V | --- | --- | V | --- | V | V | V | --- | --- | --- | --- |
| Y-Meadow Dam | --- | --- | --- | --- | V | V | --- | V | V | V | --- | --- | --- | --- |

Type of Check Dam Inspection and Maintenance V – CDFG Site Visit, I – DWR Inspection, and R – Repair
(Quelvog, 2005).

Inspection by the DSOD in September, 1996 of check dams at Bigelow, Lower Buck, High Emigrant, and Emigrant Lakes reveled that maintenance and repair work had not been completed to a level satisfactory to the DSOD and subsequently ordered the CDFG to submit a maintenance plan and schedule by January 31, 1997 (Persson, 1996). The CDFG responded in January, 1997 and indicated that the U. S. Forest Service had not renewed the CDFG special use permit for the check dams and subsequently unable to perform any maintenance or repair on the check dams and that the department did not have the funding available for maintenance (Nokes, 1997). It is unknown if any repairs to the check dams have been made since, due to on-going litigation.

Additional support in retaining the Emigrant Wilderness check dams came in 1997 when Senator John T. Doolittle of California introduced bill H.R. 1663 (105th Congress), a bill in the Senate clarifying the intent of Congress in the original Emigrant Wilderness establishment legislation in 1975 by directing the Forest Service to provide for the maintenance of all 18 check dams. The Bill simply stated:

*"The Secretary of Agriculture shall enter into an agreement with a non-Federal entity, under which the entity will retain, maintain, and operate at private expense the 18 concrete dams and weirs located within the boundaries of the Emigrant Wilderness in the Stanislaus National Forest, California, as designated by section 2(b) of Public Law 93-632 (88 Stat. 2154; 16 U.S.C. 1132 note). The Secretary shall require the entity to operate and maintain the dams and weirs at the level of operation and maintenance that applied to such dams and weirs before the date of the enactment of such Act, January 3, 1975".*

Bill H.R. 1663 was passed by the House, overwhelmingly 424 to 2 on July 22, 1997 and was then subsequently referred to the Senate Committee on Energy and Natural Resources. In a Senate Committee meeting in 1998, the Forest Service opposed the bill on the grounds that *"Congress [was] aware these structures would be included within the wilderness boundary, neither the original legislation in 1975 nor a subsequent legislation* specifically addressed these structures, or provided an exception to the general prohibition on structures in the 1964 Wilderness Act" and were "... concerned about the implications of language that might require reconstructing facilities inside wilderness. These activities, even if conducted by a non-Federal entity, would still be subject to the provisions of the Endangered Species Act, National Environmental Policy Act and other environmental laws" (Senate, 1998). The Forest Service testimony erroneously reported that Congress did not address the check dams in the enabling legislation. In the original report for the 1974 Emigrant Wilderness enabling Act, a congressional committee noted that "Certain small weirs and flow dams are present, but are essentially unnoticeable ... the weirs and small dams will likewise by retained" (HR, 1974). This statement was again referred to by the Senate Committee during hearings on the proposed Bill. Even the Forest Service at the time of the original enabling legislation agreed with the low impact of the check dams, in "... that they can be provided for within the administrative provisions" (HR, 1973).

Due to inaction on the Bill in the 105th Congress by the Senate, Representative Doolittle introduced a modified Bill H.R. 359 (106th Congress) on January 19, 1999, renamed the Emigrant Wilderness Preservation Act of 1999. The Bill required maintenance and operation on check dams at Cow Meadow, Y-Meadow, Huckleberry, Long, Lower Buck, Leighton, High Emigrant, Emigrant Meadow, Middle Emigrant, Emigrant, Snow, and Bigelow Lakes. The meadow maintenance dams and check dams at Yellowhammer and Red Can Lakes were not directly incorporated into the bill; however, given the consent of the State of California and the party performing the maintenance and operation of the check dams, those omitted check dams could be added. In addition, the Bill further defined those entities eligible for maintaining and operating the check dams and the responsibilities of the Secretary of Agriculture, including the prohibition on the use of mechanical transport and motorized equipment and also appropriated $20,000 to cover NEPA Act administrative costs incurred by the Forest Service during maintenance and operation activities by a separate party. The House passed H.R. 359 on November 8, 1999 and sent the Bill to the Senate.

Again, due to previous inaction by the Senate, the Bill was resubmitted by Representative Doolittle and by Co-Sponsor Representative Gary A. Condit as H.R. 434 (107th Congress). Once again, a Congressional report restated the original enabling legislation report: "The weirs and small dams will likewise by retained" (HR, 2001). The house passed bill H.R. 434 on September 10, 2001 and referred the Bill to the Senate. It is clear that Congress at the time of the original enabling legislation; during hearings on bills H.R. 1663, 359, and 434; and from the House passing Bills H.R. 1663, 359, and 434; the intent was to retain, maintain, and operate the check dams. However, the Bill was not addressed by the Senate in 2001 and a bill was subsequently not resubmitted in the 108th Congress.

Due to the inability of previous administrative actions and studies to resolve the fate of the check dams, the Stanislaus National Forest started a new study in January 2003 as an Environmental Impact Statement (EIS) directed specifically at the check dams that would investigate possible alternatives and environmental consequences of those alternatives. This study, the Draft Environmental Impact Statement – Emigrant Wilderness Dams, developed three alternatives: Alternative 1) Proposed Action where all check dams except Horse Meadow, Red Can Lake, Yellowhammer Lake, Bear Lake, Cooper Meadow, and Whitesides Meadow would be maintained; Alternative 2) No Action, in which no check dams would be repaired, maintained, or operated; and Alternative 3) Heritage Alternative where only the seven dams at Bigelow, Emigrant Meadow, Emigrant, Red Can, Leighton, Long, and Lower Buck Lakes eligible for the NRHP listing would be repaired, maintained, and operated (USFS, 2003).

Tom Quinn, the Stanislaus National Forest Supervisor at that time, signed a Record of Decision in December 2003 in which he selected a modified Alterative 1 as presented in the EIS. Quinn modified Alterative 1 by deciding to maintain the Red Can Lake check dam due to historical reasons and its eligibility for NRHP listing, to not maintain check dams at Cow Meadow Lake and Y-Meadow Dam, and modified various mitigation for the repair, maintenance, and operation of the check dams (USFS, 2003). This decision would preserve all check dams eligible for NRHP listing and others historically significant, except for Y-Meadow Dam which inundates a prior meadow where no significant lake existed and Cow Meadow Lake check dam, where the main check dam, is missing and would require complete replacement.

The Record of Decision was subsequently appealed by the Tuolumne County Board of Supervisors, the Central Sierra Chapter of Wilderness Watch/High Sierra Hikers Association, and the Central Sierra Environmental Resource Center (CSERC). The Tuolumne County Board of Supervisors was concerned that the issue of water storage was not adequately addressed, that failure to maintain all of the check dams would have unanalyzed economic impacts to Tuolumne Country, that reduction of lake levels at Cow Meadow and Y-Meadow Lakes would have the potential to reduce mountain yellow-legged frogs and Yosemite toad populations, the decision did not comply with the USFS/CDFG joint strategy, the decision did not enhance aquatic resources, and the check dams were not properly evaluated for listing in the California Register of Historic Places and NRHP. Wilderness Watch and the High Sierra Hikers Association were concerned about possible violations of the Wilderness Act and that the decision failed to meet direction found in the Forest Service Manual. The CSERC was concerned with the possible illegal use of manipulating streamflows and impacts on the Yosemite toad and mountain yellow-legged frog and that the decision failed to meet the direction found in the Forest Service Manual. All issues present in the three appeals were rejected with the Regional Office reviewing officer affirming the Forest Supervisor's previous Record of Decision.

Unsatisfied with the earlier appeal of the Record of Decision, the High Sierra Hikers Association and Wilderness Watch filed a civil case in U. S. District Court, California Northern District on August 20, 2004, alleging the Forest Service "*violated federal laws by deciding to maintain, repair, or operate*" check dams within the Emigrant Wilderness and "*by preparing a deficient analysis of the environmental impacts of doing so*" and to present the U.S. Forest Service from maintaining or operating any of the check dams (HSHA v. USFS, 2004). In a November 2004 response to the complaint brought forward in the suit, the USFS stated the High Sierra Hikers Association has not "*exhausted its administrative remedies*" and that the suit should be "*dismissed for its improper venue*" in a District Court area not encompassing the Emigrant Wilderness (HSHA v. USFS, 2004).

On January 6, 2005, California Trout, Inc.; Tuolumne County Sportsmen, Inc. – Mid Valley Unit; Kennedy Meadow Resort and Pack Station, Inc.; and James L. Phelan filed a motion to intervene in the case "*on the grounds they are environmental and conservation organizations whose members will be directly affected by the outcome of the pending action … and who further have historically and contemporaneously contributed materials and volunteer labor to maintain the dams*" (HSHA v. USFS, 2005). The Interveners stated they "*have maintained said dams in conjunction with the USFS by contribution of materials and volunteer labor … alleged that plaintiffs* [HSHA] *amended complaint raises what are essentially philosophical issues relating to wilderness management … High Sierra Hikers Association lacks standing to bring the present action for failure to participate in the administrative process … and failure to exhaust administrative remedies* [and that] *Wilderness Watch lacks standing to bring the present action because it is merely a 'storefront' organization headquartered in Oregon lacking any actual stake in the outcome other than an abstract interest in environmental causes*" (HSHA v. USFS, 2005).

Additionally, the California Department of Fish & Game (CDFG) filed as an intervener on February 18, 2005 as "*California's "trustee agency" for public trust resources, including fish and wildlife*", as "*the trustee for fish and wildlife affected by the Forest Service's challenged Decision,*" and that "*no other party can adequately protect this interest*" (HSHA v. USFS, 2005). The court granted intervener status to CDFG on April 5, 2005 with no opposition from the existing plaintiffs, defendants, or existing interveners.

As the Northern District Court of California agreed with the defendants (USFS and interveners) motion to dismiss for the improper venue (location) and the failure of the plaintiffs (HSHA and others) to exhaust administrative remedies, the Court transferred the case to the Eastern District of California on April 8, 2005 (HSHA v. USFS, 2005) and dismissed the High Sierra Hikers Association from the case due to it's failure in exhausting administrative remedies, such as the appeal process.

Once the case was transferred to the Eastern District in Fresno, Wilderness Watch filed an amended complaint withdrawing its claims alleging violations of the National Forest Management Act, added additional claims under the National Environmental Policy Act, and added Pacific Rivers Council (PRC) as a Plaintiff (HSHA v. USFS, 2005). Specifically, Wilderness Watch added new claims in that the USFS violated the NEPA Act in its Joint Strategy Memorandum of Understanding (MOU) with the

California Department of Fish and Game and PRC as a Plaintiff due to group's previous experience in river related matters. The Court granted the NFMA claims withdrawal, denied the additional NEPA claims as moot, and denied the addition of PRC due to the organizations failure to participate in earlier administrative processes on October 21, 2005 (HSHA v USFS, 2005). On October 28, 2005, Wilderness Watch filed another complaint, this time alleging NEPA violations and *"the existence and operation of the dam structures has negatively impacted member's enjoyment of peace and solitude"* (HSHA v. USFS, 2005).

The case is yet unresolved as of June, 2006 and the controversy will surely continue. As delays continue in resolving the maintenance and operation of all 18 check dams, further illegal vandalism and decay due to the severe winter weather present in the Emigrant Basin take its toll on the check dams. If these issues cannot be resolved soon, it is likely that many of the check dams will deteriorate significantly beyond reasonable repair and the region will have lost another historical connection to our past and an important recreational fishery in the high Sierra will be impacted.

# REFERENCES

A Bill to Designate Certain Lands as Wilderness, Public Law 93-632, January 3, 1975.

Boss, Elmer R., 1947, *Check Dams – Water and Fish Conservation*, California-Magazine of the Pacific, June, 1948.

Burghduff, A. E., 1930, *Investigation Upper Cherry Valley Area*, Interoffice Correspondence.

Burghduff, A. E., 1933, *Cherry Creek Development – Historical*, personal writings.

California Department of Fish and Game (CDFG), 1971, *Y Meadow, Bear, and Huckleberry Lakes Check Dams – Stanislaus National Forest*, Memorandum.

California State Chamber of Commerce (CSCC), 1947, *Report of the Stream Flow Maintenance Committee on the Stanislaus National Forest Check Dam Survey (Emigrant Primitive Area)*, August 17-24, 1947.

CSCC, 1950, Central Valley Council Leighton Resolution.

California Wilderness Act of 1984, Public Law 98-425, September 28, 1984.

Conners, P. A., 1980, *National Park Service National Register of Historic Places Inventory – Nomination Form for Federal Properties*, Stanislaus National Forest.

Conners, P. A., 1986, *Historical Component, Emigrant Wilderness Dam Study, in Water Control Structures in the Emigrant Wilderness, Study Report*, USDA Forest Service, Stanislaus National Forest, Summit Ranger District, Tuolumne County, California, August 1989.

DeGraff, J. V., 1988, *Geologic Investigation of Groundwater in Horse Meadow and the Effect of the Existing Check Dam, Summit Ranger District, Stanislaus National Forest*, 2880 Geologic Resources and Services.

Division of Safety of Dams (DSOD), 1972, *Inspection of Dam and Reservoir in Certified Status*, Inspection Forms (Bigelow, Lower Buck, and High Emigrant Lakes).

Dunn, L., 1973, *Emigrant Basin – Streamflow Maintenance Dams*, Tuolumne County, California Department of Fish and Game Memorandum.

Farley, J., 1933, Letter to Mr. S. B. Shaw, USFS Regional Forester, San Francisco (May 22, 1933).

Gualtieri, 1988, Letter to Blaine Cornell, SNF Forest Supervisor, Re: Emigrant Wilderness check dams, (November 14, 1988).

High Sierra Hikers Association et al. v. United States Forest Service et al. (HSHA v USFS), 2004, Complaint, 04-3478-IS.

HSHA v USFS, 2004, Answer to Amended Complaint, Civil No. 04-3478 SI.

HSHA v. USFS, 2005, Amended Points and Authorities in Support of First Amended Motion, Civil No. 04-3478 SI.

HSHA v. USFS, 2005, Answer of Interveners to Amended Complaint, Civil No. 04-3478 SI.

HSHA V. USFS, 2005, California Dept. of Fish & Game's Motion to Intervene as Defendant, Case No. C 04-3478 SI.

HSHA v. USFS, 2005, Order Granting Defendants' Motion to Dismiss Plaintiff High Sierra Hikers and Transferring to the Eastern District of California, No. C 04-03478 SI.

HSHA v. USFS, 2005, Ps' Notice and Motion for Leave to Amend Complaint, Case No. 1:05-CV-00496-AWI-DLB.

HSHA v. USFS, 2005, Order Granting in Part and Denying in Part Plaintiff's Motion for Leave to file Second Amended Complaint, Case No. 1:05-CV-00496-AWI-DLB.

HSHA v. USFS, 2005, Second Amended Complaint, Case No. 1:05-CV-00496-AWI-DLB.

Leighton, F. W., 1930, *Development Plan for Fish Culture in Stanislaus National Forest*, personal writings.

Leighton, F. W., 1931, *Construction of Cherry Creek Check Dams in Stanislaus National Forest*, personal writings.

Leighton, F. W., 1931, Reply letter to M. M. O'Shaughnessy, (May 29, 1931).

Leighton, F. W., 1931, *Statement Showing Construction Cost of Check Damming Five Lakes at the Headwaters of Cherry River*, Section added after 1934 – date unknown, personal writings.

Leighton, F. W., 1931, *Two Seven Man Crews were Organized to Build Check Dams on the Five Selected Lakes, in the Stanislaus National Forest*, personal writings.

Leighton, F. W., 1933, *Memorandum on Trout Propagation in Relation to the Establishment of Civilian Conservation Camps*, Tuolumne County Chamber of Commerce Fish & Game Committee, (May 4, 1932).

Leighton, F. W., 1933, Letter to Major John Farley, (July 19, 1933).

Leighton, F. W., 1935, Letter to J. R. Hall, Stanislaus National Forest Supervisor, (July 27, 1935).

Leighton, F. W. 1939, *Check Dams and Conservation*, personal writings.

Leighton, F. W., 1948, *Check Dams & Stream Improvements*, personal writings.

Leighton, F. W., 1949, *Valve Settings for Check Dams*, Stanislaus National Forest, (August 17, 1949).

Leighton, F. W., 1949, Letter to Allen Miller, Stanislaus National Forest Supervisor, (September 8, 1949).

Leighton, F. W., 1950, *Suggested maintenance and repair or improvement of present check dams to adequately serve the purpose for which intended*, personal writings (3/25/1950, document has been added to with dates as recent as 1955).

Leighton, F. W., 1950, Letter to J. C. Fraser, California Division of Fish & Game District Fisheries Biologist (October 5, 1950).

Leighton, F. W., 1956, *Check Dam Detail on Certain Locations*, personal writings.

Leighton, F. W., 1963, *Historic Emigrant Basin*, personal writings.

Leighton, F. W., 1963, *Check Dams in Emigrant Basin*, personal writings.

Leighton, F. W., 1963, List of the Many Inspection Parties who made a trip into the Emigrant Basin, personal writings.

Leighton, F. W., 1969, *Stream Flow Maintenance in Emigrant Basin, Stanislaus National Forest*, personal writings.

Leighton, F. W., 1971, Letter to Tuolumne County Sportsmen, Inc., (June 10, 1971).

Leighton, F. W., 1972, *Clavey River*, personal writings, (January 27, 1972).

Leighton, F. W., 1977, Letter to Frank J. Waldo, Stanislaus National Forest (June 6, 1977).

Leighton, F. W., 1978, Letter to Stanislaus National Forest Service (April 27, 1978).

Lewis, R. C., 1956, *Emigrant Basin Trip, Intraoffice Correspondence*, California Department of Fish and Game.

Mann, C. C. and Plummer, M. L., 1995, *Noah's Choice, The Future of Endangered Species*, Knopf Publishing Group.

Marovich, S., 1977, *Fred William Leighton*, in Chispa: The Quarterly of the Tuolumne County Historical Society, v. 16, n. 3.

Mills, T. J., 1974, *Lower Buck Lake Streamflow Maintenance Dam*, California Department of Fish and Game Memorandum.

Mills, T. J., 1975, *Emigrant Basin Streamflow Maintenance Dams*, California Department of Fish and Game Memorandum.

National Park Service (NPS), 1938, *Recreational Use of Land in the United States, Part XI of the Report on Land Planning*.

Needham, P. R., 1933, *A Brief Report on Observations on Trip to Cherry Creek Stream Improvement Project, September 20th-24th, 1933*, U. S. Bureau of Fisheries (now U. S. Fish and Wildlife Service).

Needham, P. R., 1934, *Cherry Creek Check Dams Aid Fish – A New Method of Stream Improvement for the Natural Propagation of Trout*, American Game, March-April issue.

Needham, P. R., 1947, *Dams Threaten West Coast Fisheries Industry*, Oregon Business Review, v. VI, n. 6.

Nokes, G. D., 1989, Letter to Blaine Cornell, Stanislaus National Forest (March 30, 1989).

Nokes, G. D., 1989, Letter to Blaine Cornell, Stanislaus National Forest (October 26, 1989).

Nokes, G. D., 1997, *Lower Buck Lake Dam, No. 1-25, Bigelow Lake Dam, No. 1-26, High Emigrant Lake Dam, No. 1-27, Emigrant Lake Dam, NIJ (Tuolumne County)*, California Department of Fish and Game Memorandum.

O'Shaughnessy, M. M., 1931, Letter to Leighton, City and County of San Francisco, Department of Public Works, Bureau of Engineering, (May 4, 1931).

Persson, V. H., 1993, *Inspection of Dams within the Emigrant Wilderness Area*, Tuolumne County, Division of Safety of Dams Memorandum.

Persson, V. H., 1996, , *Lower Buck Lake Dam, No. 1-25, Bigelow Lake Dam, No. 1-26, High Emigrant Lake Dam, No. 1-27, Emigrant Lake Dam, NIJ (Tuolumne County)*, California Division of Safety of Dams Memorandum.

Potter, T., 1952, Results of meeting held March 21, 1952, at U. S. Forest Service Headquarters, Sonora, Regarding tentative plans for stream flow maintenance dam construction in Stanislaus National Forest for 1952 and future years.

Powell, B. E., 2000, Letter to Mr. Robert Hight, CDFG Director, (November 8, 2000).

Quelvog, B., 1986, *Memorandum: Emigrant Wilderness Streamflow Maintenance Dams*, California Department of Fish and Game, (February 19, 1986).

Sizes, Inc., 2005, Miner's Inch, http://www.sizes.com/units/miners_inch.htm.

State Chamber of Commerce (State CC), 1932, *Field Trip Objective Study of Check Dams to Aid Trout Propagation as Demonstrated on the Cherry River Check Dam Project*, (September 4, 1932).

State CC, 1932, *Record of Field Trip by the Statewide Fish and Game Commission of the State Chamber of Commerce to Study the Check Dam Idea as Demonstrated by the Cherry River Check Dam Project*, (September 9, 1932).

Stockton Daily Evening Record, 1939, *Check Dams Prove Value in Aiding Trout, Improving Grazing*, (March 13, 1939).

Supernowicz, D. E., 1988, *Determination of Eligibility for Streamflow Maintenance and Check Dams within the Emigrant Wilderness, Stanislaus National Forest*.

Tuolumne County Fish and Game Association (TCFGA), 1934, *Annual Report – Board of Directors, for the year ending December 31, 1934*.

Tuolumne County Historical Society (TCHS), 1989, Letter to Herb Hahn, Summit Ranger District, (April 3, 1989).

Tuolumne Group of the Sierra Club (TCSC), undated, *Position on Removal of Emigrant Dams*.

United States Congress, House of Representatives (HR), 93rd Congress, 1st session, 1973, *Designation of Wilderness Areas, Part III, Hearings before the Subcommittee on Public Lands of the Committee on Interior and Insular Affairs on H. R. 5422 and Related Bills*, Serial No. 93-5.

HR, 93rd Congress, 2nd Session, 1974, *Designating Certain Lands as Wilderness*, Report 93-989.

HR, 106th Congress, 1st Session, 1999, *Emigrant Wilderness Preservation Act of 1999*, Report 106-425.

HR, 107th Congress, 1st Session, 2001, *Emigrant Wilderness Preservation Act of 2001*, Report 107-201.

United States Congress, Senate, 93rd Congress, 1974, *Designating Certain National Forest Wilderness Areas in California, Colorado, and Montana*, Report 93-1043.

Senate, 93rd Congress, 1974, *Proposed Wilderness Areas: Hearing before the Subcommittee on Public Lands of the Committee on Interior and Insular Affairs on S. 29, S. 110, S. 111, S. 216, S. 331, S. 332, S. 600, S. 601, S. 777, and S. 3020*, March 19, 1974.

Senate, 93rd Congress, 1974, *Designating Certain National Wildlife Refuge Lands as Wilderness*, Report 93-1287.

Senate, 105th Congress, 1998, *Dams in Emigrant Wilderness, Stanislaus National Forest, California*, Report 105-321.

U. S. Forest Service (USFS), 1969, *A Proposal – Emigrant Wilderness, Stanislaus National Forest, California*, USDA Forest Service.

USFS, 1979, *Emigrant Wilderness Management Plan, Stanislaus National Forest*.

USFS, 1989, *Water Control Structures in the Emigrant Wilderness – Environmental Assessment*, Assessment #F118902, Stanislaus National Forest, Summit Ranger District, Tuolumne County, California.

USFS, 1989, *Water Control Structures in the Emigrant Wilderness – Study Report*, Stanislaus National Forest, Summit Ranger District, Tuolumne County, California.

USFS, 1989, *Water Control Structures in the Emigrant Wilderness – Environmental Assessment*, Record of Decision and Finding of No Significant Impact, Assessment #F118902, Stanislaus National Forest, Summit Ranger District, Tuolumne County, California.

USFS, 1998, *Emigrant Wilderness Management Direction Environmental Impact Statement*, Stanislaus National Forest, Tuolumne County, California.

USFS, 2002, *Emigrant Wilderness Management Direction*, Stanislaus National Forest, Tuolumne County, California.

USFS, 2003, *Draft Environmental Impact Statement, Emigrant Wilderness Dams*, Stanislaus National Forest, Summit Ranger District, Tuolumne County, California.

USFS, 2003, *Emigrant Wilderness Dams, Environmental Impact Statement, Record of Decision*, Stanislaus National Forest, Summit Ranger District, Tuolumne County, California.

Wilderness Act, Title 16 U.S.C. 1131-1136.

Wilson, M.E., 1956, *Emigrant Basin, Stream Flow Maintenance Dams*, Department of Fish and Game, Region 4.

Wilson, M. E., 1958, *Stream Flow Maintenance Dam – Emigrant Basin – Annual Inspection Trip: August 18 to 22, inc., Intraoffice Correspondence*, California Department of Fish and Game.